Typeset by Jonathan Downes,
Cover and Layout by SPiderKaT for CFZ Communications
Using Microsoft Word 2000, Microsoft Publisher 2000, Adobe Photoshop CS.

First published in Great Britain by CFZ Press

CFZ Press
Myrtle Cottage
Woolsery
Bideford
North Devon
EX39 5QR

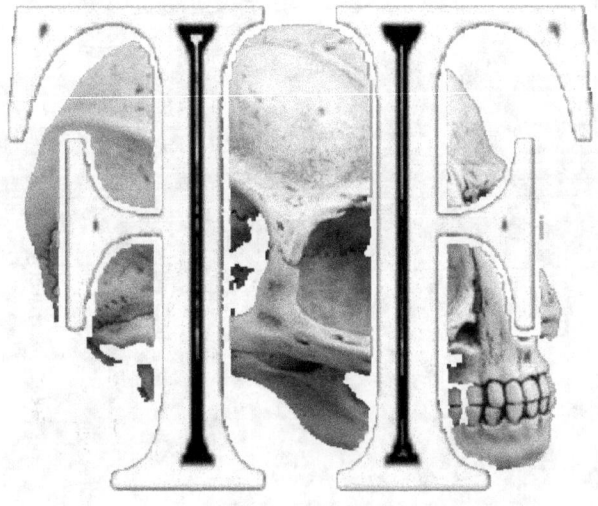

© CFZ MMXVII

All rights reserved. Without limiting the rights under copyright reserved above, no part of this publication may be reproduced, stored in or introduced into a retrieval system, or transmitted, in any form of by any means (electronic, mechanical, photocopying, recording or otherwise), without the prior written permission of both the copyright owners and the publishers of this book.

ISBN: 978-1-909488-50-2

Dedication

For her tolerance, encouragement and sheer common sense,
this book is dedicated to my dear wife, Ann Allan

Acknowledgements

I wish to express my heartfelt thanks and appreciation to the following people whose assistance, knowledge and talents helped to make this book possible.

Ann Allan, Stuart Beattie (who, at the time of writing the original MS was the Rosslyn project director), Jim and Anne-Marie Lochhead, (Mediums) Mairi Tognin (Medium), Ian Shanes (Medium), Adrian Turpin, (Medium), Patrick McNamara (Medium), Karl Fallon (Medium), Bill Downie, (musician and researcher), the late Stephen Hodge (psychologist and hypnotherapist), Nathan Surea, (acoustic therapist) Robin Budge (paranormal researcher), Chevalier John Ritchie Kt. MTS, (Militi Templi Scotia media officer), Jim Munro (Masonic and Rosslyn expert), Andrew Hennessey (musician and paranormal researcher), Rev James Collier (a.k.a The Apostle James) and Mr Marcel Leroux a dowser from Connecticut in the USA.

Special Thanks

Special thanks goes to Mr Richard T Cole, for designing the excellent new cover art for this version of the book.

Contents

	Page
Dedication:	3
Acknowledgements:	5
Authors note:	11
Introduction:	13

Part One
The Background

Chapter 1: A Brief History of Rosslyn Chapel.	19
Chapter 2: The Sinclair Family.	25
Chapter 3: The Knights Templar.	31
Chapter 4: The Chapel Interior and One of The Mysteries.	39
Chapter 5: Rosslyn and the Templar Connection.	45
Chapter 6: Rosslyn and The Holy Grail.	49

Part Two
The Esoteric Dimension

Chapter 7: The First Evaluation.	57
Chapter 8: Signs and Sounds	59
Chapter 9: The Choristers.	65
Chapter 10: Why Mediums?	71
Chapter 11: Secrets and Treasure	75
The Apprentice Pillar	77
Chapter 12: The Lady Chapel.	79
Chapter 13: The Devil's Chord	81
Chapter 14: The Third Revelation.	85
Chapter 15: Into the Vortex.	93
Chapter 16: The Baphomet.	97

Part Three
On the Other Side

Chapter 17: Stargate Rosslyn?	103
Chapter 18: What Lies Below?	105
Chapter 19: Through the Doorway.	107
The picture of the altar	107
First impressions	108
Chapter 20: The Second Communication.	113
Chapter 21: The Red Light	121
The Apostle James sends a warning.	123
The Dream	124
The Next Message	126
Epilogue:	129
Suggested further reading and references:	133

'Reality is an approximation'.

Plato

Author's note:

Over the years there have been several books written about Rosslyn Chapel, the most recent seem determined to undermine any possibility that this very special building is anything more than a stone church, albeit highly detailed and elaborate, and nothing more. This work confronts this rationalist stance head on and presents startling new evidence suggesting just the opposite. From the outset it should be clear that two quite distinct histories are applied to Rosslyn Chapel. One is the official version insisting that the Chapel is nothing more than a place of simple piety and worship, while the other is a much more esoteric shadow interpretation with immense implications, the histories are not interchangeable and there are very few points of convergence.

While it is obviously much safer to stay with the official version of events, this does not even come close to explaining the many possibilities, mysteries and enigmas that surround and permeate this incredible and beautiful medieval building. For this reason, although mindful of the traditional explanation, we shall follow the rather more convoluted route of the shadow interpretation, for it is only within this less obvious path that we shall ever come close to uncovering the truth behind the breathtaking secret which is concealed in this church. I wish to express my unreserved gratitude to Mr Stuart Beattie, the former Rosslyn project director, for his invaluable help and assistance over the years in allowing this series of experiments and evaluations to take place. I should point out that although he was very helpful and generous regarding access to the Chapel, Mr Beattie holds no views or opinions one way or the other on what is discussed in this book. In addition, I also wish to thank all those who assisted in the project because their first hand opinions and observations helped shape, and indeed are part of, this book.

I should make clear that although there is a 'Questing Prize' of some £5,000 (approx $7,800) awarded by the late actor, comedian, author and esotericist Michael Bentine for anyone who solves the true riddle of the Chapel, it has not as yet been claimed, and it is doubtful that it ever will. The work described here was carried out in the spirit of seeking the truth, discovery and knowledge and not as an attempt to secure any reward. In addition, due to the nature of both the puzzle and the building itself, there may well be more than one message concealed within the ancient weathered stones, so the prize is likely to remain unclaimed in the foreseeable future except by those either foolish or arrogant enough to think that theirs is the only possible explanation.

Introduction

If ever there was an example of Sir Winston Churchill's famous quotation referring to Russian foreign policy, as *'a puzzle wrapped in a mystery inside an enigma'* applied to a building, then surely this building must be Rosslyn Chapel. Over the years fevered speculation over this medieval structure has fuelled a series of quests to uncover what, if any, arcane secrets and codes may be encoded within its design. These quests have involved everything from the straightforward and robust, i.e. drilling directly into the vaults through the flagstone covered floor of the Chapel, to one notorious incident when an entirely unauthorised attempt to bore into the vaults was made from a steeply sloping field at the east end of the building. This cavalier incident led to the Chapel trustees acting to prevent further unauthorised attempts like this being attempted. They bought the land!

On the other hand there has also been considerable learned historical and archaeological research and debate about the images and patterns carved into the stonework. It is notable (but hardy surprising) that the more intrusive archaeological endeavours have all been rebuffed, although several ultrasound ground scans have been carried out with considerable success. In addition there have been attempts to employ very different and subtle types of questing techniques using the talents of psychics and mediums, and although these methods are officially dismissed they appear to have had more success than the more conventional and traditional, and it is to these alternative methods that we apply ourselves.

While it can be argued that all places of worship are, by nature, in a sense supernatural or otherworldly, as we shall see, in the case of Rosslyn Chapel this assertion just might be literally true. The theories expounded and words written about this small Midlothian Chapel are legion, but until fairly recently the interest in the building and its legends was confined to a relatively small band of people. They tended to be academics, historians and members of various quasi-religious and mystical groups, e.g. the *Freemasons*, the *Rosicrucians* and the *Militi Templi Scotia (*MTS*)*, who are a relatively modern, (18th century) Scottish variant on the legendary and near mythical order of warrior monks, the Knights Templar.

Ownership of the Templar inheritance has been claimed by a variety of groups and organisations and there are a series of Masonic degrees, beginning with the Royal Arch and continuing through The Preceptory and Cryptic Council, all of which are rituals invoking

Templar imagery and traditions. Additionally there have been other, less worthy groups who claimed to invoke the Templar name, its inheritance and its code of honour, among them the OTO, or '*Ordo Templi Orientis*' and the more recent, but much more venal and avaricious, '*Order of the Solar Temple*'. Both of these groups were more concerned with enacting rituals and quasi-magical ceremonies than promoting chivalric values, particularly the OTO, which included the notorious late Victorian era magician Aleister Crowley among its members. In the case of the Solar Temple, which was in fact organised and operated more like a cult, the lives of several of its adherents ended in mass suicide at the whim of it founder rather than initiation into anything genuinely worthwhile. Having said that, the Knights Templar themselves were also reputedly involved with heretical and magical practises and we shall look at some of these charges and their implications later in this book.

In the past few years however, even prior to the arrival of the astonishingly successful novel and film, 'The Da Vinci Code', the building and its grounds have become a magnet for thousands of people from all over the world. Each person had their own reasons for going there, although the overall impression is that they are all on a pilgrimage, but first a word about *The Da Vinci Code* and its remarkable penetration into public awareness. Although the Chapel was already quite well known due to earlier books such as 'The Holy Blood and The Holy Grail' and 'The Hiram Key', plus its companion work, 'The Second Messiah', it was not until after the publication of the by now almost ubiquitous 'Da Vinci Code', that widespread interest of the building really ignited. Precisely why this should be the case is puzzling, but perhaps it is because this particular work, being one of fiction, has a much wider appeal than more serious works designed primarily to educate and provoke thought, but ultimately, of course, to entertain. The reaction of the churches, especially the Roman Catholic Church, in leaping forward to denounce what is after all presented as a work of fiction is also surprising, but given its fierce traditionalist conservatism in these matters this is perhaps predictable.

On the other hand their reaction could be described as illogical; why decry a fictitious work suggesting that Jesus Christ married Mary Magdalene while promoting belief in a supernatural male entity who, with no physical contact, supposedly caused a human woman to become pregnant with his offspring, and what is more the offspring performed acts of necromancy, magic and sorcery. It is curious that the reason Christ was put to death on the cross was not because he was a troublemaker, which, although this was a civil offence it was not one deserving execution. Instead it was because he was deemed as a *'malificus'* i.e. a magician, something that, along with sedition or anything else deemed to be a crime against the state, did attract the death penalty; specifically the degrading, agonising and often protracted method of crucifixion.

The Romans were well aware of just how spectacularly brutal this was and deliberately used it to discourage any acts of insurrection or rebellion against the state. In fact, so agonising was this particular form of execution that it has become embedded in our language as 'excruciating' taken from the Latin, 'ex-crucis', or 'of the cross'. It is sometimes assumed that through the death of Christ that this form of execution was the sole invention of the Romans, but it was also an approved method of execution in Islamic culture and also in ancient Japan and Burma. Even today it still occurs in Saudi Arabia and other countries in the Middle East. Sadly the brutal Islamic State (sometimes called ISIS) terror group also uses it.

Staying with the 'Da Vinci Code', after her death Mary Magdalene was canonised as a saint by the Catholic Church and her relics were originally venerated at the abbey of Vézelay in Burgundy. She rapidly gained a huge, almost cult-like following, and later, in 1279 at Saint-Maximin-la-Sainte-Baume in Provence, France, where her remains were apparently relocated, they attracted such enormous throngs of pilgrims that an earlier shrine was rebuilt as a great Basilica. From the mid-thirteenth century on, this building became one of the finest Gothic churches in southern France. This part of the Magdalene legend helps corroborate the theory that she did in fact travel to France, with or without Christ, to create the beginnings of an entire alternative Grail mythology. Perhaps ultimately all churches should be grateful for the increased attention, because they will ultimately benefit as a result as it indicates that deep down in the human psyche there still seems to be an unrequited thirst for spiritual comfort that only they can supply.

Finally, in relation to the subject of this book, i.e. Rosslyn Chapel, the manner in which it is presented in the film of *The Da Vinci Code* is quite inaccurate and misleading. Although the exterior shots are fairly accurate, the depiction of the crypt and what it contains are, to say the least, fanciful. The apparently large side room off the north wall of the crypt, a feature that plays a part later in this account, is entered by the two main characters and is in fact no bigger than a large closet and there is no manuscript laden vault hidden beneath it; nor is there an elaborately carved, symbol rich ceiling above it.

In spite of appearances to the contrary, the reasons for the resurgence of interest in the Chapel, 'Da Vinci Code' notwithstanding, are, in the last analysis, all related to one thing. This is a hunger for spiritual gnosis tied to the enduring enigma, whether real or imaginary, created around the arcane knowledge encoded in the myriad of ornate carvings that adorn the building. Plus, and perhaps more importantly, the intense speculation as to what, if anything, is hidden in the vaults deep below the Chapel. If the stories are to be believed, Sir William Sinclair, the third and last Prince of Orkney, when he inaugurated the building of the Chapel intended to create an enduring legacy, an inheritance immortalised in stone, something tangible that was there for all to see and would carry ancient, occluded knowledge down through the generations. However, as we shall soon discover, sacred and spiritual items may not necessarily be the only artefacts secreted away in the vaults, tunnels and chambers which are reputed to lie below the Chapel, perhaps there is an even more bizarre claimant for this honour.

It is possible that access to knowledge and artefacts dating from the very dawn of humanity lie hidden there, and perhaps it may be better for the human race that they are never uncovered. As we shall also discover when there is a treasure, particularly one that is for whatever reason regarded as potentially dangerous, the people who hide it frequently appoint a guardian or guardians of one kind or another to prevent its discovery, for some secrets are perhaps best kept concealed and never meant to be found. While this interpretation of the building and its carvings may be true, they are not necessarily unique. The alchemist, Fulcanelli, in his book *La Mystere des Cathedrales* (The Secrets of the Cathedrals), which first appeared in 1926, made this claim for all the great Gothic cathedrals like Notre Dame and Bruges, asserting that they contained the secrets of alchemy hidden in their myriad carvings and beautiful geometric proportions.

Was Sir William a human guardian then, privy to knowledge that possessed virtually limitless power and even now, more than five centuries later, still has the potential to shake the human race to its very core? Did he also believe that what he concealed had no place on this earth and for the sake of the human race had to be placed beyond the reach of fallible human beings in a location where they could not possibly gain access to it? Did he, thorough his unique access to highly specialised sources of esoteric, ages old information, create a 'gateway' into an impregnable strongroom designed to hold this item? The knowledge entrusted to Sir William was in many ways highly dangerous, especially to him and his family. Ignorance and stigma bordering on hysteria concerning witchcraft was rife in Scotland in the 15th century and the very hint that he was privy to such heretical and esoteric information was a certain death sentence to both him and his family irrespective of how powerful he was. We shall discuss this possibility, but perhaps we should first look at some of the other, more obvious aspects of the building.

The fabric of the Chapel could have been desecrated or destroyed on many occasions, most notably by Oliver Cromwell who was not noted for his sensitivity, and also during the Protestant Reformation in Scotland. As we shall see later, the worst damage from this era took place during the Civil War when Cromwell's troops, commanded by General Monk, held Rosslyn Castle under siege and stabled their horses in the Chapel building. The fact that he chose to spare it further harm may be due to its Masonic connections. It is known that Cromwell was a Master Mason and it is likely that knowledge of Rosslyn Chapel and its links with the craft of Freemasonry was well known even then, and we shall return to these links in detail shortly.

The damage inflicted in the 16th century by a local Protestant mob during The Reformation could also have been considerably worse, but it is likely that after their initial display of zealotry they lost interest. The knowledge encoded in the designs is not intended for the uninitiated; rather, it takes the form of images, allegories and precise measurements taken from diverse beliefs and traditions. Masonic, Templar, Alchemical and Pythagorean teachings, all are represented here. Indeed it is likely that there is even more information hidden among the rich and ornate carvings; the more one looks the more one sees and feels. There is an indefinable impression of serenity combined with a great, yet indefinable, power here, quite separate from the contemplative silence found in most churches; it is an almost tangible sensation. In my experience there is only one other place that has a similar aura and mystique and this is at the supposed birthplace of Jesus Christ located beneath the Church of the Nativity in Bethlehem, where the sense of being in a place of immense spiritual importance is literally breathtaking.

Part I
The Background

Chapter 1
A Brief History of Rosslyn Chapel

The area surrounding the Chapel is steeped in Scottish history, and the nearby Roslin Castle, which is still owned by the Sinclair family, predates the Chapel by over a century, and was strategically important during the Scottish wars of independence. *(Note: there are a number of spelling variations relating to Rosslyn and the nearby village of Roslin, these varied with the era and usage, all are correct.)* A battle, 'The Battle of Roslin', was fought there in 1303; when a band of eight thousand Scotsmen defeated a thirty thousand strong force of English soldiers during a series of three engagements fought over twenty-four hours. There is reputedly, and perhaps predictably, the ghostly image of a mounted Black Knight, which has been seen by several motorists while driving past the surrounding area.

The Chapel itself also has its own tales of spectres, and in this case the sightings have mainly been of monks, although other entities have also been reported. The most impressive of these sightings was in the crypt and reputedly featured a monk praying at the altar situated below the crypt window, and surrounded by four knights. There are also claims that several mummified lords of Rosslyn lie on biers in the Chapel vaults shrouded only in their armour. The strangest, but from our point of view the most significant legend attached to the Chapel, concerns events that allegedly occur upon the death of Sir William of Rosslyn's direct descendents; when the entire Chapel allegedly lights up as if it was on fire. The following verses taken from *The Lay of the Last Minstrel* by the famous Scottish poet and author Sir Walter Scott, appears to emphasise two of these very features.

> *'It seem'd all on fire that Chapel proud,*
> *Where Roslin's chiefs uncoffin'd lie,*
> *Each Baron, for a sable shroud,*
> *Sheathed in his iron panoply'.*
> *'Blazed battlement and pinnet high,*
> *Blazed every rose-carved buttress fair*
> *So still they blaze, when fate is nigh*
> *The lordly line of high St Clair.*

Reports of strange and anomalous lights in and around the Chapel are even now occasionally still reported, and the comment concerning the covering of the naturally mummified bodies is also significant. There is yet another connection between Sir Walter Scott and Rosslyn; he was so fascinated by the Chapel that at his beautiful home, Abbotsford House near Melrose on the Scottish borders, he had certain stone carvings from the Chapel recreated in wood on the library ceiling. These include the heavily embossed cube-shaped pendants in the Lady Chapel and the angels depicted playing musical instruments. In a way this represents a full circle, since the original masons who constructed Rosslyn centuries earlier converted wooden patterns specifically approved by Sir William into stone. The official explanation is that he had a passion for medieval architecture, but is there another less obvious reason? Even then did the intuitive and creative side of Sir Walters's nature prompt him to suspect that there was much more in the decoration than met the eye, and that by incorporating the cryptic carvings into his own home that he would, in some way, become part of the mystery?

When one also factors in the origins of the name, Sinclair, we are confronted with at least one explanation for this phenomenon of ghostly luminescence. As we shall see, in one version the surname Sinclair originates from St. Clair, a name that in turn evolves from Sanctus (or Santos) Claros, which, intriguingly, literally means 'Holy Light'; this will be dealt with in detail in a later chapter. Are the lights reportedly seen in the Chapel somehow directly related to the surname of the family? On a slightly different tangent, there is one particular tale that, as we shall see in the second part of the book, has another strange synchronicity with the Chapel itself. This is the legend that if a certain trumpet note is sounded while standing on a specific step in the castle, a great treasure will be revealed.

The legend goes on to make a similar claim for the Chapel and coupled to the reports of the building spontaneously illuminating upon the death of any of Sir Williams's descendents, there may even be a grain of truth in this. It has been argued that all cathedrals and churches, especially medieval examples, were specifically designed to first create, then enhance, the impression of contact with the divine and as we will see, this is precisely what Rosslyn Chapel does. This, perhaps vital, secret was revealed during a still ongoing series of investigations and evaluations that began in 1998 and, as we shall discover, it may be only the beginning.

Although this is ostensibly no more than an exceptionally ornate small church, closer examination reveals that it may be more, a great deal more. As we have seen, the reasons for its construction are themselves still unclear, although there are several plausible theories. There is a suggestion that the Chapel was intended as the retro-choir of a much larger cathedral, but what is certain is that it was built at the instigation of Sir William Sinclair between 1446 and 1490. It is often assumed that construction was begun in 1446, but it appears that although the original charter for construction was granted in that year by the Vatican, the only body that could authorise the construction of collegiate churches like Rosslyn, building did not actually begin until 1456. The work was almost certainly jointly overseen in its initial stages by Sir William and his close friend and mentor, the exceptionally able and intelligent Sir Gilbert Hay who for many years had been librarian to the French court.

It has also been suggested by a chronicler of Sinclair family history, Father Richard Augustine Hay (1661 - c.1736), who was their chaplain and a descendant of the aforementioned Sir Gilbert, in 1700 when he completed a three-volume chronicle of the Sinclair family, that the Chapel was the end result of a desire felt by Sir William to demonstrate to God that he was deeply grateful to Him for the benefits he and his family had enjoyed during his lifetime; or perhaps he was simply just buying a little bit of insurance. It is entirely likely that Father Hay, whose mother eventually married Sir James St Clair, belonged to Clan Hay, the scions of Yester Castle, which is only a few miles from Rosslyn and as we shall discover may even be linked to it via an extensive, and largely natural, tunnel and cavern system. It is also vital to appreciate that while Father Hay did an excellent job of gathering and compiling all the information concerning the Sinclair family from both written records and oral traditions, if he made any mistakes then there is little that can be done to correct them, because all the original documentation was irretrievably lost.

During its construction Sir William employed the services of skilled masons from all over Europe and the original habitation at Roslin was created prior to construction of the Chapel in order to house the work force. It has also been suggested that the crypt in Rosslyn also served this purpose prior to better accommodation becoming available. It is a mark of Sir William's determination to have the best possible workforce, that he paid the most skilled and talented craftsmen the then princely sum of £40 per annum and the less skilled £10 per annum. Although convention says that the structure should have been part of a cathedral, or that it may only have been intended as a place for private family worship, this does not appear to be the case.

Convention also says that when Sir William died in 1484 he was buried within the unfinished Chapel and as a result the intended and much larger building was not completed, although there is compelling evidence suggesting that it was never intended to form part of such a structure. On a technical point it should be noted that there was no wood used anywhere in the original construction of the Chapel, everything was crafted in stone, even the roof, the construction of which is the largest example of its kind in Scotland. The wood, where it exists, was introduced much later when the baptistery was constructed in the mid-19th century.

When the backlash against Roman Catholicism picked up speed and eventually culminated in The Reformation, (sometimes called The Protestant Reformation) the future of the Chapel was in doubt in particular because, at that point, the Sinclairs stubbornly refused to renounce their deeply held Catholic beliefs and conform to the prevailing Protestant orthodoxy. This did not impress the elders of the Protestant movement and in 1589, firebrand reformer John Knox's brother, William, was publicly castigated for baptising the then extant Lord of Roslin's child in Rosslyn Chapel, which was by then viewed as *'A house and monument of idolatry and not a place appointed for teaching the word and ministrations of the sacraments'*. In 1590 the same Protestant hard liners forbade Rev George Ramsay, the minister of Lasswade, a small town near Rosin village, from burying Oliver Sinclair's wife in the Chapel.

In 1592, the same unfortunate Oliver Sinclair was warned to destroy all six altars in the Chapel on pain of excommunication, and on the 31st of August 1592 the aforementioned Rev George Ramsay reports that, *'The altars of Roslene were haille demolishit'*, and from then on the Chapel fell into disrepair and ceased its function as a place of sanctuary, prayer and worship. Eventually the Sinclairs, displaying a remarkable degree of pragmatism, officially converted to Protestantism although they continued to practise their Catholic beliefs in private. It is likely that if they had not done so they would have forfeited much of their land and property and irrespective of position, time or place, loss of prestige and money is always an excellent persuader.

Following other relatively minor acts of vandalism at the hands of the mob, the Chapel remained abandoned until 1736, when Sir James Sinclair glazed the windows, which had formerly been covered with wooden shutters, for surprisingly this had not been done before, repaired the roof and had the floor re-laid with flagstones. In 1861, James Alexander, the Third Earl of Roslyn (sic), felt that since the political and religious climate had changed slightly, services should be restarted and to this end employed an Edinburgh architect, one David Bryce, to oversee the necessary restoration work. During this time all the altars were rebuilt with an additional altar established in the crypt, and the ornate carvings in the Lady Chapel were repaired and renovated, but there is still some damage evident in what is perhaps one of the most mysterious features in the entire Chapel, namely the hundreds of enigmatic carved stone cubes (213 in number) located in the ceiling of the Lady Chapel. The Bishop of Edinburgh carried out the rededication in April 1862 and the sermon was preached by the Bishop of Brechin, (a town on the north east coast of Scotland). The rededication of the building and the new altars was not intended for the restoration of Catholic worship, but instead the Episcopal strain of Protestantism.

No doubt the present congregation is irritated by the constant theorising and speculation surrounding their place of worship, but as is often the case in circumstances like this familiarity breeds contempt. A similar situation exists when one considers the Pyramids of Egypt. If you ever have the opportunity to visit these magnificent ancient monuments you will find that the local people are so used to them that they have become completely blasé. The visitor is rightly overawed by their sheer physical presence, their gigantic, almost surreal stark beauty and what they represent, but the locals however seem totally indifferent to them except as a means of extracting money from the awe-struck tourists on their whistle-stop tours. So, to a lesser degree we find the same situation at Rosslyn where there is now a small café and gift shop staffed by employees and volunteers of the Rosslyn Trust. The most recent addition is a dedicated visitor centre complete with a video presentation and ticket office which leads directly into the Chapel grounds. To be fair these alterations are, along with the tourists, necessary to help secure the funds required for the upkeep and maintenance of the ancient building.

Remarkably, in the 20th century the Chapel came very close to closure once again during World War II, when, in 1942, it was noted that very few worshippers turned out for Sunday service, in one case only two, and this it was felt was a disproportionate waste of money in a time of national hardship. A zealous local official named Robertson wrote to the government and the letter was eventually seen by Lloyd George, who at the time was the Minister for Fuel. The government minister, both Welsh and a devout Christian, wrote to the Secretary of State for Scotland expressing the view that there was much greater spiritual value in keeping the Chapel open than closing it to save a few pounds, and thanks to him it remained open.

However, in the 1950s, after cleaning the internal carvings of discolouration and lichens etc with an ammonia solution, a coating of magnesium fluoride was applied as a preservative wash to the surfaces of the now cleaned carvings. This had the effect of sealing them and trapping moisture and soluble pollutants inside the stonework thereby creating conditions of high humidity within the Chapel, and in 1995 a recommendation was made to remove the coating and allow the stonework to dry out naturally. This was, to say the least, a lengthy process that lasted several years.

As well as creating this undesirable situation, the particles in the wash also partially filled in and obscured some of the finer details in the carvings, and regrettably this may never be successfully removed. Finally, in 1997, a steel canopy was erected over the roof to allow the entire building to dry out naturally and this had the additional advantage of allowing visitors easy access to a walkway high on the steelwork, where they could safely examine the normally inaccessible external carvings and statuary on the structure. However, in July 2010 when the programme of renovations on the weather-eroded sections of the building was completed, the canopy was removed and the Chapel, once again, looked as it was originally intended.

Chapter 2

The Sinclair Family

The Sinclairs, whose family motto is *Commit thy work to God*, did not just suddenly appear fully-fledged just prior to the construction of Rosslyn Chapel, although they have undoubtedly become uniquely and inextricably linked with this medieval building. But their origins, like the purpose of the Chapel, are not straightforward. One version of the genesis of the Sinclairs, and in particular their name, suggests that the present line originated at the end of the first millennium and since most surnames derive from events, places, occupations and characteristics, the Sinclairs were no different.

Their name is apparently adopted from the village of St Cler (or Claire), a small Norman settlement that still exists close to the junction of the Seine and Epte rivers. This practise is still true to some extent here in the United Kingdom, where a person's occupation or town of origin is still frequently appended to their name, i.e. family names like 'Stirling', 'Scotland', 'England' and 'English' are quite common. It is also common practise in the Middle East e.g. Saudi Arabia, for a family to incorporate, at least in part, the name of their town, village and even country of origin, e.g. the family name Al Bishi derives from the town of Bisha, Al Taruti from Tarut and Al Malawi from the country of Malawi. In this last instance it is likely that the ancestors of the family had originally been brought to Saudi Arabia as slaves centuries ago.

According to tradition, the first Sinclair was one Captain Rollo 'the Walker', a Norseman, who took his nickname from the fact that he was too large to ride the small Norse ponies and therefore had to walk everywhere. Evidently Rollo, (or Hrolf as his Viking kin knew him) was engaged in fighting with the Franks as part of the Viking invasion of Normandy, where he defeated the garrison of St Cler Castle and King Charles the Simple offered him a treaty if he would stop harassing his subjects. The terms were straightforward enough; if he would agree to do this and in the process convert to Christianity, King Charles would give him his daughter's hand in marriage, make him 1st Duke of Normandy and award him the title of Rollo of St Cler. The custom of intermarriage, or marriages of convenience, is a long established and civilised method of cementing relationships, allegiances and contracts. It is a dynastic practice still regularly employed among royal families and business empires, and whatever else, Rollo (or perhaps his advisor) was no fool and could see the long-term implications and advantages, so the treaty was duly signed in 911 AD at the castle of St Clair-sur-Epte. The Sinclair surname has had a wide range of spelling variants, twenty five at one count, dating from 1261 with Seincler, Santoclair in 1407, Singlar in 1454, Santclere in 1545, to Sinkaller in 1692.

The Sinclair's Rosslyn connection dates from the very beginning of the second millennium when another William Sinclair, this time William the Seemly, who, in 1057 along with another knight, Ladislaus Leslyn, had accompanied Margaret, a Saxon princess, from Hungary to Scotland where she married King Malcolm Canmore. This journey is depicted in a carving on the south wall of the Chapel and reputedly shows Margaret carrying a cross while sharing a horse with Ladislaus, who is also credited with founding the Leslie family in Scotland. It is also claimed that, displaying the dualism featured in many carvings in the Chapel, this image also depicts the traditional Templar icon of two knights sharing one horse, which, in turn, symbolised their vows of poverty, a vow that, when the Templar order became astonishingly wealthy, was eventually cast aside.

The cross borne by Margaret in the carving was part of her wedding dowry and depicts a holy relic given to her by the King of Hungary, in this case allegedly part of the true cross, the Holy Rood sometimes called the 'Black Rood', in other words part of the actual cross on which Jesus Christ suffered the unimaginable agonies of crucifixion. It is also important to realise that there were two 'Roods', one that was part of her dowry and another that was a personal possession. This much smaller artefact was a silver crucifix in which was set a sliver of wood also claimed to have been part of the cross of Christ's martyrdom. It remained with her throughout her life and we shall return to the problematic subject of religious relics later in this chapter. Following her death, Queen Margaret was interred at Dunfermline Abbey and eventually canonised by Pope Innocent IV in 1249, an honour that, because of her many charitable and pious acts, was evidently well deserved.

In gratitude for services rendered, King Malcolm made William Sinclair cupbearer to the by now Queen Margaret, and was awarded 'life rent' (a lifetime lease) of Rosslyn. This was later changed to full ownership, or 'free heritage', in return for additional services to the king. To receive this extra royal favour the unfortunate William was killed in battle while defending the Scottish borders against attack by the English, so it was his family and descendents who enjoyed the benefits. His son Henri, the first Sinclair to be born in Scotland, fought in the First Crusade and was one of the knights present when Jerusalem finally fell to the Saracens. It is not clear whether he was also at the final battle in the Holy Land when the enigmatic Knights Templar, to whom the Sinclair family are traditionally linked, were finally forced to relinquish the last Christian stronghold at Acre. There were several reasons why Acre was the last redoubt of the Templars, not least being its strategic location near the coast and fact that it was the site of their treasury. When they were finally defeated the contents of the Acre preceptory vaults went with them to their new headquarters on the island of Cyprus.

However, there are another two variations on how the Sinclair name originated, and in these accounts the Sinclairs, who, like all Normans, were descended from Vikings, for reasons unknown appropriated the name of a dead, expatriate Scottish mystic. Evidently Rollo's own lineage was from Rognvald the Mighty, Jarl (prince or earl) of Orkney and of More and Romsdhal, two areas of Norway. The extended family, whose name, More, was originally adopted from the area of the same name, had gradually moved south from Orkney with Rollo's forces at the close of the tenth century and following Rollo's treaty with the Norman ruler, King Charles, had settled in Normandy. In this account, the name Sancto Claro(s) came from a Scottish hermit and mystic named St William Sancto Claros.

Unfortunately, how he acquired this name is not recorded, but it may have derived locally from his pious and mystical lifestyle. St William evidently spent his days, as befitted a holy man, in meditation and prayer and as such was largely blameless, but to his ultimate (and fatal) cost he became scandalised by the liaisons and affairs of a local titled lady and complained to all who would listen. This holy and rather ingenuous man was warned to stop making his observations but he did not, which resulted in his murder; he was beheaded at the request of the affronted lady. For reasons that are far from clear the More family took his name, but whatever the reason it is yet another link to the enigmatic disembodied heads that appear in various guises throughout their history, and are also linked to the Knights Templar.

Another variation on the origins of the Sinclair name comes from the academic, Andrew Sinclair, who is a direct descendant of Sir William, in his book entitled, simply, *Rosslyn*. According to Mr Sinclair's research, Sancto Claros died in the 6th century and St Gregory of Tours later recorded his life and death in the 11th century. Evidently another document from later in the 11th century suggests that Sancto Claros was in fact Greek and had been converted to Christianity by St Paul. This alternate version also suggests that Sancto Claros and six colleagues met their death at the hands of tribes indigenous to the Lectoure area of France while tying to convert them from their pagan beliefs. This was hardly surprising due to the considerable antipathy created by attempting to foist a foreign and unwelcome system of worship on the locals, plus the fact that, due to their Christian beliefs, the would-be evangelists refused to make sacrifices at the Temple of Diana. The author was evidently able to view the coffin of Sancto Claros and was surprised to see it adorned with Gnostic and Masonic carvings.

This is unusual, but in the context of the knowledge later enshrined at Rosslyn Chapel should not come as any great surprise, for it appears that certain branches of early Christianity were deeply involved with various strains of Gnosticism. This was perhaps due to the emerging Christian Church gradually subsuming and consolidating compatible strands of belief from other teachings into its own system of belief and understanding. The constant exposure of these early missionaries to a variety of beliefs did, however, lead to a number of them finding these alternative teachings more appealing than those of their own, to the point where they secretly adopted and practised them. This policy adds weight to a variety of theories and speculation suggesting that the story of Christ and his well-documented birth, life and death, was the last in a series of attempts to define the theme of a dying and rising God; in effect the ultimate victory for the cult of Sol Invictus. It is highly likely that a number of esoteric and long-lived mystery schools sprang from this rich and kaleidoscopic blend of mysticism.

The Sinclair family was also said to be represented in 1314 at the pivotal Battle of Bannockburn when Scotland, under the leadership of King Robert the Bruce, finally achieved independence from England. It was after this battle that King Robert awarded another William Sinclair the prestigious position of Bishop of Dunkeld. It should pointed out that, although confusing, as with many families there are different branches of the original family group who obviously share many Christian names. Nor can it be overstated just how important religion was in this era; truly, the church and state were absolutely as one. Kingship, politics and religion, it was the one effective way of keeping control of the population, although to be fair, the common people were just as avidly and unquestioningly religious and superstitious as their lords and masters.

The practice of combining church and state within a family was commonplace, and even encouraged, among the ruling classes until the 17th and 18th centuries and it was accepted as the norm for titled families to have offspring (always male) placed in both ecclesiastical and/or parliamentary positions, all to preserve their privileged status quo. In reality it was all about absolute power and control, and in many ways it still is. The Sinclair family continued to play an active part in many key areas of Scottish political and religious life for many years, but as time passed and the warring nations of the British Isles grew united, diplomacy became the preferred method of resolving disputes, and they slowly faded into the background. The current family of the Sinclairs of Rosslyn are for the most part academics and less inclined to wield a sword or axe.

Returning to the matter of the second relic, the Black Rood, this relic was a richly embossed, cruciform reliquary set with diamonds and topped with an ivory carving of Jesus Christ. It contained yet another fragment of the cross of Christ and is one of the many objects supposedly secreted way in the Chapel vaults. Most importantly, it is also one of the few artefacts that might actually be there, a view held by the Milti Templi Scotia. It should be noted that this relic was taken into battle by King David III in 1346 during a foray into England and was lost, but it reappeared shortly afterwards in Durham Cathedral where it remained on display for some considerable time as an object of veneration. It was taken from there circa 1530 by Sir Simon Sinclair and since it was apparently not returned, it remained in the possession of the Sinclair family. However, perhaps it is more fitting to say that it was restored to its rightful place among the treasures of Scotland rather than wrested from Durham Cathedral as a spoil of war. In fact the practise of taking objects of veneration, into battle, be they religious artefacts or otherwise, although perhaps foolhardy, was far from unusual.

However it is no more extraordinary than someone choosing to wear a St Christopher medal when travelling and was done for exactly the same reason, i.e. to invoke the protection of a supernatural agency. Even those with no discernable religious beliefs still follow this and similar practises, which indicates that these customs may work at a deeply subconscious level as a form of sympathetic magic. Curiously this is also one of the methods used to invoke the agency that drives chaos magic. The desire to invoke supernatural blessings and protection on a mission or quest through a fetish or totem object, which is in reality what all religious artefacts are, is found in many non-Christian cultures; particularly in the animistic beliefs still found among the nations of Africa and the tribes of Native Americans. Here, it is still common for someone embarking on a journey to first consult the map then ask for the protection of tribal power objects and/or the spirits who guard the pathways in an example of spiritual 'belt and braces'.

Bizarrely, it was reputedly a concept shared by Adolf Hitler when he decided to appropriate the Spear of Longinus, (sometimes called the Spear of Destiny) from the Hofburg Museum in Vienna in an effort to somehow harness its supposed supernatural power to assist in his self-appointed mission to inflict his ideology on the world. It is the same weapon supposedly used by the blind, veteran Roman Centurion Gaius Cassius, to pierce the side of Christ as he hung, dying on the cross. Neither was it an accident that for the same reason Hitler reputedly launched quests to find many other ancient religious artefacts and it has been suggested that his deputy, Rudolph Hess, was extremely interested in Rosslyn Chapel.

Precisely what his interest was has never been satisfactorily explained, but it may be connected to his firm belief that, amongst other things, Rosslyn was a Grail Chapel. It might be sheer coincidence, but the Spear of Destiny was kept in St. Catherine's Church in Nuremberg during the most successful phase of Hitler's military campaign. However, in October 1944, after his fortunes declined and the Allied star rose in the ascendant, the spear and other artifacts were removed to a specially constructed underground bunker in the same city. Six months later, on April 30th, 1945, exactly eighty minutes after American forces took possession of both the bunker and the spear Adolf Hitler died, apparently by suicide although that is still hotly debated, in the Fuhrer-bunker deep beneath the streets of Berlin.

In the years prior to the ultimate triumph of the Nazi party in Germany, it is known that in 1930 Rosslyn Chapel was visited by a member of the Thule Society, the German occultist, Dr. Karl Fuchs, who was at the time also on a visit to the Edinburgh Theosophical Society. Fuchs later insinuated that he had been specifically instructed to visit the Chapel. During his visit he was accompanied by someone who signed the visitor's book only as D. Hamilton. It is widely assumed that this was none other than the Duke of Hamilton, the same Duke of Hamilton who Rudolph Hess reportedly tried to make contact with following his fateful flight to Scotland in a Messerschmitt fighter plane at the beginning of the Second World War. It has been suggested that Hess had been duped into making this flight through the efforts of the British Intelligence services who had fed him with false information regarding certain pro-German sympathies within sections of the British Government.

Both the Thule Society and the very similar Vril Society were rabidly nationalistic esoteric groups created to exploit and encourage the huge upswing in interest in a range of mystical and magical beliefs, which accompanied the meteoric rise of Aryanism and the Nazi party. Another prominent Nazi who attempted to create his own pseudo-Templar organisation was of course the leader of the SS, Heinrich Himmler, who spent huge sums of government money reconstructing the fortress at Wewelsberg in Westphalia. Himmler hoped to create a spiritual centre for his SS whom he looked upon as a form of evolved Templars, and we shall return to this subject in more detail later. That Hitler and his associates did not succeed in their unholy quest may be due to reasons of infinitely greater subtlety and strength rather than the hell mouth of raw firepower.

Chapter 3

The Knights Templar

In spite of claims to the contrary, it is more likely that the Sinclair family, if not having representatives as *bona fide* members of the Templar order, were at least well disposed towards them rather than overtly hostile. The fact that they spoke out against the order of warrior monks after their proscription was more likely due to the fact that, displaying remarkable pragmatic stoicism, the Sinclairs were determined to distance themselves from any links with the organisation and remain aloof from any possible recrimination that might have affected their tenure over their property and lands. This cannot have been easy for them because the Sinclair family was devoutly and avowedly Roman Catholic, a fact that nearly cost them dear during the harsh, grim, humourless years of the Protestant Reformation in Scotland.

Although they did adopt the Protestant faith and eventually became hereditary Grand Masters of the Masonic Order, this was another prime example of the pragmatism that influenced, and continues to influence, the rich and powerful. As far as the Sinclairs were concerned it indicates that irrespective of how sincere their beliefs may have been, when push came to shove and their religious inclinations might have cost the dynasty its influence, property and lands, money beats mantras every time. There is a deep rooted belief that the Sinclair family were connected in one way or another, either tacitly or overtly, to the Knights Templar and since Rosslyn Chapel has been mooted as a shrine to this mystical order it is appropriate to include a short evaluation of the Templars. However, once again like the Sinclair family and the Chapel, there is more than one version of the story, which continues to demonstrate the dualistic Gnosticism surrounding almost every aspect of this most enigmatic of orders.

According to accepted wisdom, around 1118 AD two French knights, Hughes de Payens and Godfrey of St. Omer, were the instigators and founders of the Knights Templar, or 'The Poor Knights of Christ and the Temple of Solomon' as they were originally known. They travelled to the Holy Land and approached King Baudouin, (or Baldwin) the 1st, the King of Jerusalem, taking with them the blessing and sponsorship of St. Bernard of Clairvaux, a prominent member of the Cistercian order of monks and the spokesman for all Christendom in this era.

Ostensibly, their intention was the protection of pilgrims travelling to and from the holy land after the first Crusade, from assorted Saracen thieves and bandits. Evidently King Baudouin, himself a former crusader, was delighted at the prospect since it relieved him of this responsibility and he promptly presented them with a wing of his palace to use as their headquarters. However, what happened next is open to conjecture.

The numbers of the fledgling order were swiftly made up to nine in total, then for the following nine years virtually nothing is known. All that is certain is that no new members were admitted, and although they may have made occasional token patrols on the pilgrim routes, the original nine were seldom seen to leave their quarters. This may have been connected with the fact that the quarters so generously donated by King Baudouin were constructed on the ruins of Solomon's Temple. The conjecture is that the warrior monks appear to have spent their time digging under the temple looking for, well, what exactly? There are many theories, but as with so much concerning this secretive group no one is completely certain. The best available evidence suggests it was a mixture of treasure, both material and spiritual. Details of the items secreted there are mentioned in The Dead Sea Scrolls found at Qumran, especially on the copper scroll. The material treasure is more easily quantifiable in terms of precious metals and gemstones etc., but the spiritual, what could that have been? From all of this speculation one thing is certain, the founding of the order of warrior monks had originally very little to do with protecting pilgrims and a great deal to do with gathering information and treasure, which leads to the question, who sent them and why? After the initial period of nine years, in 1127, some of the Templars returned to France to consolidate their position and Hugues de Payen was elevated to the rank of the first Templar Grand Master. During this time most of the rules governing their appearance, dress and even their diet were drawn up, e.g. they were not allowed to shave and so they cultivated magnificent, full, beards. This may have been at a pious whim, but it also neatly mirrored the Islamic custom that men should have beards and may have been an early indication that some Muslim influences were taking hold. Coincidentally, it also proclaimed their masculinity and ferocity on the field of battle, and like many similar displays of prowess can be likened to the Scottish warrior practice of baring their posteriors to opponents.

Some years later in 1139, a landmark papal bull was issued by Pope Innocent II exonerating them from compliance with any article of civil law and established their legal and social position as responsible solely to the Vatican and the Pope. It is likely that one of their original sponsors, Bernard of Clairvaux, did some serious lobbying to achieve this unique award. Some years after this in 1146, they were awarded their famous insignia of the cross pattee, which proclaimed their adherence to the teachings and ideology of Christ and their willingness to attain martyrdom should the need arise. It is worth noting that the Templars were, due to their strict discipline and religious fervour, probably the most feared and efficient fighting men in the world. Indeed their code forbade them from leaving the field of battle if they were faced with fewer than four foes per man; this kind of stricture would have guaranteed their grim determination and ferocity in battle. This trait can still be seen in modern times in the actions of such extremist groups such as Islamic State and similar fundamentalist religious zealots.

There is also the likelihood that. as with many groups who have a powerful spiritual or mystical ethos behind their cause, they may have seen themselves as more or less invulnerable to the weapons of their adversaries. This concept was sometimes found in certain Native American tribes and in more recent times with the Zulu nation in South Africa, whose extraordinary and fearless confrontations with the British Army were frequently fuelled by a mixture of the exhortations of their shamans and mood altering substances. It was also found with the Mau Mau guerrilla fighters in Kenya who, in their frequent encounters with the authorities, were likewise convinced that bullets would not affect them as long as they were unshakable in their beliefs.

Unfortunately from both their perspectives, since bullets seldom heed prayers, psychoactive chemicals or deeply held belief, this was not the case. Because of the Templars' sheer and unrelenting courage in battle they were held in high regard by their sworn enemies the Saracens, themselves fierce and well-disciplined warriors. Indeed, it was from this climate of mutual respect with the Saracens that they obtained much of their considerable knowledge of pharmacological and metalworking skills. This probably resulted in the Templars absorbing some of Islam's mystical beliefs as well, which, irrespective of their unique position, had it been generally known would not have found much favour with the church authorities, and most likely been condemned as a heresy, and we shall return to this and related crucial matters later in the book.

It would seem logical that this order of soldier-monks should be created by the Church since a military wing might be seen as a useful adjunct to religion when both church and state were, in effect, one and the same. This was particularly so of the Roman Catholic Church whose dreams of conquest and power combined with the spread of their version of absolute truth was carried out in the name of their God. Equally, the Catholic Church, if not itself actually responsible for their inception, would at least have been fully aware of the Templars and must have approved, or at least acquiesced, in their creation. However, as we shall see, it may not have been the Roman or any other church that created them and the treasure may indeed have been spiritual in nature, nothing less than the 'Lost Gospels of Christ'. The Essenes, a fundamentalist Jewish sect of which Christ himself may have been a member, reputedly wrote these along with the Dead Sea Scrolls, which were also found at Qumran.

The contents of these gospels can only be guessed at, but like the Gospel of Philip (and others) found not far from Qumran at Nag Hammadi, the contents may be potentially explosive for accepted church dogma. The manuscripts discovered at Nag Hammadi came to be known as the Nag Hammadi Gospels (or Codices) and as with the Dead Sea Scrolls, it is fair to assume that they would have presented a totally different facet on traditional teachings. This would be especially true in relation to Christ's brother, James the Just, a biblical character whose importance has been deliberately played down, and Christ's inferred intimate personal relationship with Mary Magdalene. Both these aspects of the story of Christ tend to be swept under the carpet by all the churches, and totally denied by some. It is now a commonly accepted belief in many quarters that, true or not, Christ and the Magdalene were married and had a family of their own, which brings us back to the Templars.

As an interesting aside, in 1894, the British Army in the form of Lt. Charles Wilson of the

Royal Engineers entered the tunnels originally created by the Templars and discovered several Templar artefacts. These were in the possession of one of his descendants, the late Robert Brydon, who appropriately enough until his death in 2014, was the archivist of the Templars in Scotland. Today this modern Templar offshoot is known as the *Militi Templi Scotia*, but the majority of the mystical aspects have little in common with the originals. This group conduct their rites and ceremonies within Rosslyn among other locations, and whose stated *raison d'etre* appears to be the maintenance of the Scottish nation and its chivalric traditions, although there could well be other less obvious hidden motives.

An alternative version to the founding of the order suggests that they were in existence at least four years before they knocked at King Baudouin's door in Jerusalem. There are some indications that the true inspiration behind the Templars was a shadowy organisation dating from the 7th century. This group is the *'Priory de Sion'* and the Templars may have been created as their military wing, in effect their bodyguards and enforcers. This secretive organisation, whose origins and legitimacy are still the source of much debate and conjecture, is allegedly still in existence today and has reputedly included such luminaries as Leonardo da Vinci, Robert Fludd, Robert Boyle, Victor Hugo, Claude Debussy, and Jean Cocteau amongst its Grand Masters. According to the excellent and thought provoking work, *'The Holy Blood and the Holy Grail'* by Baigent, Leigh and Lincoln, The Priory de Sion were themselves founded to promote and sustain the Merovingian Dynasty in France, the so-called 'Long Haired Kings'.

Their purpose was to return the dynasty, deposed in circa 600AD, to the French throne. This was intended as a stepping-stone to the other European royal houses and Britain was also included in this grand design; the pretenders in this case would have been the Sinclairs. We can see therefore that the Priory de Sion would be prepared to go to great lengths to obtain the finances and documented proof that it required. Again we must ask ourselves, why? There is one possible direct link between the Templars and the Priory. The uncle of their main sponsor, St. Bernard of Clairvaux, was André de Montbard, one of the original nine knights who belonged to an organisation called the *'Ordre de Sion'*...is there a connection? The Merovingian dynasty were, apart from allegedly possessing magical powers, (which is in itself not especially noteworthy since various royal houses actively encouraged and fostered similar rumours about themselves), allegedly blood descendants of Christ and the Magdalene. The magical connection is, as we shall see later, also an attribute associated with Rosslyn's founder, Sir William Sinclair. This then is the rationale behind the Priory de Sion and their quest via the Knights Templar to discover what was secreted away beneath the temple in Jerusalem.

Following their initial nine years in Jerusalem, the Templars rapidly expanded with wealthy families vying with one another to have at least one of their sons accepted by the order. Their acceptance was normally accompanied by a generous donation of money, property or land and sometimes all three, which quickly led to the Templars becoming both powerful and remarkably wealthy, a fact that contributed to their eventual downfall. As it expanded, the Templar order regularly transported money and supplies between Europe and Palestine and as a result developed an efficient form of banking system. They are also credited with creating the first system of 'promissory notes' or cheques. The traveller would purchase the note at one of the main Preceptories in Europe by depositing the cash equivalent and for a small fee retrieve their currency once the journey to the Holy Land was completed.

Eventually, and in spite of several ferocious crusades, the Holy Land was steadily returned to Muslim rule and with the fall of the final outpost at Acre, the reason for the very existence of the Templars became tenuous and unfocussed. However, by this time, the order was so incredibly wealthy and powerful that it owed its allegiance to no one except the Papacy. They had strengthened their grip on power by lending vast amounts of money to several European Royal houses, notably King Philippe le Bel (the Fair) of France who was particularly indebted. This resulted in the order receiving the King's considerable enmity.

Apart from owing the Templars a fortune there was a well-grounded fear that the order was preparing to set up its own homeland in southern France, thereby threatening both the stability of the country and King Philips own position. Because of this and of course a fair amount of jealously, the King, with the acquiescence of his placeman Pope Innocent VI drew up a string of charges against the order. These were designed, mindful of the Templars unique relationship with the Papacy, to ensure action had to be taken. Among the list of charges were, Satanism, blasphemy, sodomy, teaching women to abort, idolatry and as we shall see, the worship of a head (sometimes referred to as a demon) called 'the Baphomet'. It is curious that many of the charges laid against the Templars were strikingly similar to accusations made against the 'fallen angels' who allegedly taught humankind many sciences.

We should perhaps be clear that unlike a similar, but somewhat less charismatic religious organisation, 'The Knights Hospitaller of St John', the Knights Templar were not universally liked, and in many cases feared. As a result of their unique social and financial position, they were, like many super rich and insular organisations, in many ways divorced from reality and effectively above any civil law and existed in a unique vacuum filled only by their own codes and rules of behaviour and conduct. Such was their disregard for convention that the expression *'as drunk as a Templar'* came into common usage and their attitude to the oath of celibacy was likewise somewhat cavalier. It is also a prime example of the old quotation that despite any number of original good intentions and their supposed piety that, 'Power corrupts and absolute power corrupts absolutely'.

They steadily devolved into an insular and supremely arrogant organisation that was not dependent on any outside assistance to function, because all their needs, both physical and spiritual, were well catered for from the various interests to which they were sole party. We should also remember that the Knights themselves were supported by lesser ranks within the Templar organisation. These were the sergeants, the men-at-arms and those purely designated to care for the spiritual needs of the brethren. In addition to this 'logistics group', as we have seen there were a large group of non-combatants who kept the knights supplied with the all the staples of food, armour, horses and clothing etc, etc, necessary to sustain them both in battle and away from the field of combat. All of these items came from within the infrastructure of farms, workshops and armouries created by the Templar order.

However all that came to a sudden end when, on the morning of Friday the 13th of October 1309, a series of raids on all Templar properties and Preceptories in France was carried out resulting in the majority of the Templars in France being captured. Interestingly, there is evidence to suggest that the previous night, the Templar fleet of 18 ships sailed from the port of La Rochelle presumably carrying the contents of the treasuries. This was the start of the superstition of Friday the 13th being unlucky; and it certainly was for the Templars. Since King Philippe's men found very little in the form of disposable wealth in any of the Templar properties, it is a fair bet that there was foreknowledge of the raids for it is inconceivable that they did not know. A powerful organisation like that must have its agents everywhere, particularly to sniff for gossip and possible leverage in the court of the King, and the only reason that they did not flee was because the did not think that there could be any possible danger to themselves, either that or it was due to their astonishing arrogance. They were after all, in their opinion, literally above the law.

The only group to benefit directly from this action were the Knights Hospitaller who were eventually awarded the Preceptories and some of the land accrued over the years by the Templar order. Of those that escaped some went to Portugal, where after being tried and found innocent of any wrongdoing, promptly reformed themselves as the 'Knights of Christ'. Some arrived in Germany where they joined the Teutonic Knights, and those who came to Scotland allegedly brought certain scrolls that are among the artefacts allegedly hidden at Rosslyn and here we have a possible source for the association of Rosslyn with the Grail. The Templars allegedly possessed the container that once housed the Turin Shroud, which was at the time an object of absolute veneration, and through its intimate association with Christ an obvious substitute for the Holy Grail. It is also one of the objects that is thought to have been removed, along with more tangible wealth, from their treasuries and brought to Scotland.

Those who came to Scotland were afforded sanctuary by King Robert the Bruce and a contingent of them fought alongside Bruce at the Battle of Bannockburn. The battle took place on the 24th of June 1314, which is also, perhaps tellingly, also the feast of John the Baptist. It is claimed by authors Robert Lomas and Christopher Knight in their book, *'The Hiram Key'*, that the Templar contingent was led by none other than Sir William Sinclair in his capacity as the Scottish Templars Grand Master. The group fought under the *'Beausant'*, which was the distinctive black and white battle flag of the Knights Templar. We shall return later to the reasons why Bruce ignored the specific instructions of a Papal Bull requesting the arrest of any Templars found and instead welcomed them. In turn, Sir William St.Clair befriended them and if the account of Lomas and Knight is accurate, i.e. that the Chapel built by Sir William at Rosslyn was intended not just as a place for family worship, but an enduring tribute and shrine to the Templar order and its mysteries, this is perhaps another tangible example of the Gnosticism embodied in the Chapel.

After seven years of imprisonment, the last of the Templar Grand Masters, Jacques de Molay, along with fellow Templar and second in command Geoffroi de Charnay, on 13th of March 1314, was eventually burned at the stake, or more precisely roasted and suffocated to an agonising death over a slow fire. In keeping with the aura of magic and the occult that still hangs over this most enigmatic of orders, it is said that before he died Jacques de Molay cursed the king and Pope Clement, calling for them to join him and account for themselves before the court of God within a year and remarkably this is exactly what happened. Less than a month later Pope Clement was dead, supposedly from dysentery and by the year's end, for reasons that are still not clear, so was King Phillip. Events like these only served to further enhance the reputation of the Templars as masters of alchemy, magic and the occult arts.

Whether they were or not is open to question, but cannot be ruled out, it is even possible that they cultivated rumours of magical practises for their own ends, which may be an example of what is now called 'disinformation' designed to conceal other nefarious practises, or was it just because they revelled in their own notoriety rather as the self-styled early 20th century magician, Aleister Crowley, relished his own epithet, *'The wickedest man in the world.'* It is said that as late as 1789, immediately following the execution of King Louis XVI, an unidentified man leapt onto the guillotine, dipped his hand in the blood flowing from the decapitated body of the king and flicked crimson droplets of it out over the crowd, shouting, *'Jacques de Molay, thou art avenged'*. The aura of magic that hung like a pall around the order still survives today and is now perhaps even more readily received. If the Sinclair family had any links with the Templar order, then it is quite possible that this included knowledge of certain magical arts, what we might now refer to as a 'practical spiritual technology' and that the various formulae for these arts is hidden in Rosslyn Chapel.

It has frequently been stated that the order was completely dismantled and quashed with the Knights arrested in France, but this is simply not the case. As we have seen, the organisation carried with it a huge network of ancillary organisations designed to support it, and the people who ran these interests were not persecuted; this unwelcome honour was reserved purely for the Knights. Another demonstrable fact corroborating the continuation of a Templar presence are the number of place names in Britain, particularly in Scotland, that incorporate the word 'Temple' in their structure, and as a rule of thumb if a place name incorporates the word 'Temple,' then at one stage it played host, or belonged to, the fugitive Templars. Examples of this are Templand in Dumfries, Templehall in Fife, and Temple, (formerly Ballantrodoch) in Midlothian. In fact there are many places throughout Great Britain called only 'Temple'. This practise is also found throughout Europe, which indicates that many members of the order, and not just the lower ranks, managed to escape the clutches of the King.

Chapter 4

The Chapel Interior and One of the Mysteries

Before we embark on the series of evaluations that took place within the Chapel we should examine the interior, for it is here that many of the clues lie. When entering the Chapel by the north side door one is not immediately aware of the sheer number of carvings decorating almost every available area of stonework, in fact the only area of the Chapel not adorned and festooned with carvings are the flagstones on the floor. Moving to the right toward the baptistery one is drawn towards the windows where the bas-relief carvings frame the stained glass and bizarrely, there is one particular image depicting a horned deity. Indeed, there is ample evidence on display within the Chapel to suggest animistic and Gnostic traditions alongside the purely Christian.

This is typical of the building and in doing so helps to corroborate the theory that it was never intended to be a church, but a scaled down copy of Herod's Temple in Jerusalem and this can be seen by comparing the floor plans of both buildings which are strikingly similar. The comparison with Herod's temple may be highly significant for another reason since, according to the existing accounts, Herod's temple had three levels below ground. The oral traditions concerning Rosslyn assert that the Chapel is as deep as it is high, (the depth is estimated at forty two feet), which may be an indication of what lies beneath ground level. This is one version of the history of the building that finds some common ground, because it is known that there are several burial vaults under the flagstones of the Chapel floor, but whether there are any additional voids under them is as yet unknown, but if the stairway leading down into the crypt is, as is sometimes claimed, a truncated version of the original, then there may be some truth in this. The belief that the Chapel is constructed on the remains of a Temple of Mithras also gains some credence based on the existence of the vaults below the Chapel; Mithraic temples were always located in caves or caverns and this may be what is there.

There have been many theories regarding the similarity of the Chapel to other ancient places of mystery and worship, including assertions that the Chapel is, depending on where the information comes from, similar to either Solomon's or Herod's Temple in Jerusalem. The most recent claim is that the Chapel is a copy of the east quire of Glasgow Cathedral, which certainly predates Rosslyn. Perhaps there is an element of truth in all of these claims, but since the main feature seems to be the number of pillars in the Chapel and the fact that, as with Herod's Temple, there are two dominant pillars, is it possible that the Chapel was built to feature specific aspects of all these places? In other words, did the builder recognise the magical resonances inherent in all of these buildings and attempt to make his own creation the embodiment of them all? Bear in mind the tradition suggesting that the Temple of Solomon was built using magical forces, specifically demons invoked by Solomon, who was claimed to be an accomplished demonologist and magician. The more one looks at the traditions surrounding the Chapel and its builder, the more one is irresistibly drawn into a world of the occult, magic and mystery.

Moving round the walls one cannot but help notice the lintels above the passageways, all of them feature rich decorations of plants and foliage, but only one example of text and this is a Latin inscription on a lintel next to the Apprentice Pillar which, in English, reads: *Wine is strong, the king is stronger, women are even stronger but truth conquers over all*. This quotation is reputedly taken from Masonic ritual, specifically the Royal Arch degree, which concerns the destruction and eventual rebuilding of the Jerusalem Temple. Over in the aisle on the west wall one can see the famous carvings of maize and aloes that were not known in Scotland at the time. It is details such as these that help corroborate the claim that one of Sir William's ancestors, Prince Henry the navigator, had been in North America decades before Christopher Columbus allegedly discovered the continent. This account is worth looking at as it is one of the many legends that have grown up around both the Sinclairs and the Chapel and we shall therefore return to this later in the chapter.

Another feature that becomes obvious is the large number of engrailed crosses and angels that adorn the walls, the engrailed cross being synonymous with the Sinclair family. Perhaps the engrailed design is not there for purely decorative reasons and forms a deliberate and intrinsic part of the structure, especially on the ceiling of the crypt below the Chapel. This is a feature we shall return to in part two of the book. Standing in the main part of the building and glancing up at the barrel-vaulted ceiling, one sees bands of rich decoration comprising stars, flowers and roses; always the rose, symbol of the Virgin Mary, concealment, secrecy and of course the Holy Grail. Perhaps the most lavishly decorated section of the Chapel is the now famous Lady Chapel, for this is the location of three ornate pillars and the mysterious cubes, which may hold the key to the mystery.

Of the three pillars, The Masters, the Journeyman's and the Apprentice, the only two of real note are, facing east, the 'Master's Pillar' to the far left, and to the right the now near-legendary 'Apprentice Pillar'. This is, according to Keith Laidler in his book, *The Head of God*, the hiding place of Christ's mummified head. There is some support for this hypothesis based on the results found when metal detectors were used to scan the pillar and an object possessing the approximate dimensions of a head was allegedly located inside. In a line from north to south along the centre of the Lady Chapel there are three intricately carved suspended bosses, the centre of these illustrates the nativity. Set against the east wall and again from

North to South are four small altars dedicated respectively to St Matthew, The Virgin Mary, St. Andrew and St Peter, and each altar bears a carving of the unmistakeable enGrailed cross of the Sinclair family.

One of them, the St Peter altar, is both raised slightly above the level of the other three and is not readily accessible because it is sited directly above the flight of stone steps leading down into the crypt, and for obvious reasons is also sometimes referred to as 'the high altar'. Located to the right of the Lady Chapel and immediately beside the Apprentice Pillar, originally called the Princes Pillar, are the stairs leading down to the crypt. Until a few years ago anyone descending into the crypt had to exercise great care as the stone steps were very badly worn. However, in the interests of safety, and possible claims of ruinous litigation, this defect has now been remedied. The crypt is a bare, dark room partly illuminated by the light coming through the two stained glass windows set in the east wall, although in the early morning the sunrise projects brilliant shafts of colour reflecting off both walls and visitors alike. Beneath the windows is a small altar set into the wall and on the north wall there is a door leading to a room, which may have been used to store drawings during the construction phase of the Chapel.

The walls of the crypt are sparsely adorned with a few bas-relief figures of angels and saints and a few graffiti-like technical drawings that appear to date from when it was built. It has been suggested that the crypt is older than the Chapel above it, and it is possible that one of the original entrances into the vaults was through the wall at the west end of the crypt. Before leaving this aspect of the Chapel it should be pointed out that there is an existing school of thought suggesting that the use of the term, 'Crypt', is incorrect and that this area was actually the site of the original Chapel. It is known that prior to the construction phase of the present Chapel, the floor was earthen, at least a metre deeper, and as already mentioned it also housed some of the workforce. Perhaps it also gave admittance to the natural cavern and tunnel system that is reputedly below the Chapel, it may also be a reference to the additional levels below the floor of the Chapel, but more of this later.

Henry the Navigator
Prince Henry Sinclair was born in 1345 and grew up in Rosslyn Castle and at the age of twenty four he assumed a remarkably varied range of titles including among others, First Prince of Orkney, Seventh Baron of Rosslyn, Jarl of Orkney and Caithness, Lord Admiral of Scotland, Duke of Oldenburg (in Denmark), and a total of twenty other baronies. The Orcadian and Scandinavian titles indicate the origins of the Sinclair family. That the Sinclairs were wealthy cannot be in doubt when one considers that at age thirty five, Prince Henry financed the building of a fleet of ships allegedly greater in number than the national fleet of Norway. In 1398 he set sail for Newfoundland and Nova Scotia with twelve ships, and the services of the Italian Zeno brothers as his navigators. The fleet comprised of between 300 and 600 souls including 200 soldiers, some members of the Knights Templar and a number of Cistercian monks who possessed farming skills. It is assumed that he intended to claim any land found for Queen Margaret of Norway.

The crossing was not without incident and five of the ships, along with many of their passengers and crews, were lost and when they did eventually arrive in the New World, probably Nova Scotia, they found to their surprise that many the natives spoke a number of familiar languages including Erse, Basque and Norse, which if true surely indicates that there had been many previously unsuspected visitors to these shores. Contemporary reports indicate that Henry found the native Micmac people amenable, so he and his followers spent their first winter peacefully quartered among them. During this time he explored the Massachusetts area and ordered one of the Zeno brothers, Antonio, to take the remainder of the fleet back to Orkney while he remained ashore with a group of soldiers, carpenters, shipwrights, sailmakers, knights and Cistercian farmers. The accounts taken from contemporary Micmac legends say that Prince Henry and his men built an 'island' (ship) and put 'trees' (masts) on it and with this vessel travelled further down the east coast.

Further evidence of Sinclairs' presence in the area is offered in the form of the 'Boat Stone' currently located in the library at the town of Westford, in Massachusetts. The Boat Stone is oval and approximately two feet in diameter at its widest point. It is engraved with the image of a ship resembling those of the 1300's era and also marked with distances, presumably to the voyagers' camp. The stone was discovered by a road building crew who, thankfully, did not destroy it. Another apparently affirmative artefact is the so-called 'Westford Knight', which was discovered in 1883 and depicts a European knight in armour. It is mentioned in a local reference book compiled by the Rev Edwin R Hodgeman called *A History of the Town of Westford*,. The Rev Hodgeman thought it had been carved by the native Micmac Indians. In 1950, again in the vicinity of Westford, another artefact was discovered, this time a sword believed to be Viking and dating from the 1300's. It is also recorded that a 14th century Venetian cannon was dredged up from Louisburgh harbour on Cape Breton Island and helps to indicate where Sir Henry first landed. Unfortunately, in 1400 when Henry and at least some of his men returned to Orkney, crewmen from an English fleet commanded by Sir Robert Logan murdered him. His body was taken back to the place of his youth, Rosslyn, and buried at the family Church of St Matthew. This church no longer exists, although it is believed to have been situated in the nearby cemetery and it is assumed that his body was exhumed and re-interred in a vault below Rosslyn Chapel, but as with so much of the Rosslyn mythos there is no solid evidence for this.

Nova Scotia and the Money Pit

It is Prince Henry's sojourn in Nova Scotia that illustrates another bizarre legend associated with the Sinclairs and the Templar treasure. It has been speculated that during his exploration of the coastline bordering Nova Scotia, he and his men went ashore at Oak Island, constructed the legendary Money Pit and hid part of the cargo that they had brought from Orkney. It has been suggested that this cargo comprised a fraction of the near mythical treasure of the Knights Templar, although the evidence for this is purely circumstantial. According to existing accounts of the Money Pit, it was first located accidentally in 1795 by three boys playing in the area, and from the outset its discovery has generated a remarkable amount of interest and several serious and expensive exploratory expeditions. At a depth of two feet the pit consisted of a layer of stones and at ten feet the first of a series of oak beam platforms was discovered, each successive platform was ten feet below the previous one.

In 1849 the Truro Company, a company specialising in drilling, bored augur-bit holes near the existing excavation and struck another oak platform at 154 feet down and the drill bit fell a further foot on to another platform and on through 22 inches of metal scraps which included an old watch chain. A few feet below this, more wood appeared - both oak and spruce - along with yet more metal scraps. Other excavations uncovered small pieces of parchment with writing on them; unfortunately these were for the most part very fragmented and unreadable. To date over $2 million has been spent on various projects investigating the Money Pit, but so far there has been no success in either discovering its purpose or what it contained, although it has always been assumed that this was the source of the gold panned from the nearby Golden River.

Chapter 5

Rosslyn and the Templar Connection

It is frequently argued that there is no connection between Rosslyn Chapel and the Knights Templar, but in the light of the available evidence this is unlikely, because the same voices that strongly deny any Templar connection will simultaneously admit to a strong Masonic connection and the two organisations share many common traditions. However, coincidence and speculation do not form the basis for truth, so we should look at what evidence there is. There are several apparent connections between the Sinclair family and the Knights Templar; one is said to be the marriage of Catherine de St Clair to Hugues de Payen, one of the founders of the order, and the fact that the first Templar preceptory constructed outside the Holy Land was on land belonging to the Sinclair family at Temple (Ballantrodoch).

It should also be remembered that up until the Reformation in Scotland the Sinclair family were devoutly Roman Catholic, as by the very nature of their calling were the Knights Templar. The marriage of Catherine de St Clair to one of the founding knights does however make one question the validity and seriousness of the vows of celibacy taken by the members of the order who were, in effect, monks, and as such were bound by the same laws that still affect all monks, nuns and priests today. These vows were originally enacted to prevent any priestly families having claim on property that either belonged to, or had been appropriated by, the Church. The stated reason was naturally expressed in far more spiritual terms i.e. that since Jesus was not married then, therefore, neither should his instruments be here on Earth: they would in effect be 'married' to the Church. This is still seen, particularly in convents where the nuns are considered to be 'Brides of Christ'.

The Scottish link was particularly useful following the Templar dissolution in 1307, when many refugee knights made their way to Scotland. They were made welcome and given sanctuary by King Robert Bruce who did not heed the Papal Bull (directive) that was issued instructing that they be given no succour and immediately arrested because, apart from the ongoing hostilities against the English army, he had been excommunicated for the killing of

John (The Red) Comyn, and as a result the Bull was not proclaimed, so technically it did not apply. In England the situation was only slightly different and the knights who chose to remain there were normally arrested and sentenced to a short period of penance in a suitable monastery. On the other hand, some were left alone without let or hindrance; much depended on the views and inclinations of the local authorities.

The murder of John Comyn took place in February 1306 at Greyfriars monastery in Dumfries and by all accounts Bruce, who was not yet the King, did not succeed at the first attempt. After stabbing his adversary, Bruce left him alone on the flagstones in front of the monastery's high altar to die, but some monks took him to a side room to minister to his wounds. When Bruce heard of this he immediately returned to the church and physically dragged Comyn back to the altar where he repeatedly stabbed him again, this time making sure he was dead. A close relative of Comyn tried in vain to save him, but was himself killed by Christopher Seton, who was Bruce's brother in law.

It was bad enough to have murdered Comyn, but the fact that the deed was done in a church was all the more unusual, because at that time churches were places of sanctuary. This situation was respected by even the most hardened soldiers and mercenaries, who, it might be reasoned, might possibly be in need of the facility themselves at some point. It is clear then that Bruce, who was crowned King only six weeks later, either had good reason to kill his enemy, or he cared little for the niceties and traditions of sanctuary. It is possible that Bruce detested Comyn for his placatory stance towards the English King Edward, or he considered him as a possible contestant in his quest for the throne.

Following their ferocious dissolution in France and their subsequent flight to various locations, Templar vessels travelled to both the East and West coast England and also to Scotland, where testimony of their presence can be seen in the gravestones in the Church at Kilmartin that are emblazoned with Templar symbolism. In addition, as we have already seen, it is claimed that the Templar Grand Master who at the time was Sir William St.Clair, led the Templar battle group at the Battle of Bannockburn. There is also evidence to support the claim that the Templar legacy was carried on by families other than the Sinclairs, viz. the Setons and the Sandilands, who, along with the Montgomeries, were powerful and extremely influential Scottish dynasties. Another possible factor linking the Templars to Rosslyn Chapel may come from the undeniable Masonic imagery used in the decoration in the building and the strong likelihood that certain Templar rites were absorbed into Masonic ritual, particularly in the case of the Third Degree and the stories surrounding the Apprentice Pillar strongly reflect this. There is also the fact that the Sinclairs were eventually made hereditary masters of the Masonic Lodge.

This privilege has powerful resonances with the year, 1441, five years prior to the inauguration of Rosslyn Chapel when King James II of Scotland made the Sinclairs *Patrons and Protectors of Scottish Masons*, a post that was hereditary; that said it is important to make the distinction between speculative and operative masons. Speculative masons are those who meet in today's Masonic lodges and operative masons who were the men that shaped and assembled the rough stones into buildings and who formed the original guilds and lodges of practical masons. There is, however, another and more recent connection from 1838 related to an oil painting entitled *A Templar Knight in Roslin* (sic) *Chapel* by one R.T. McPherson, depicting a bearded man in a white tunic, hose and gauntlets wearing a white cloak. On his head there is a cap with a tall, red and white feather and the tunic and cloak are both emblazoned with the familiar red Templar cross, the Croix Pattee. Over his left shoulder (facing) in the background is the unmistakable image of the apprentice pillar, and to his right, next to a crucifix, there is a skull. Unfortunately there is no record of the identity of the figure. The inclusion of the skull in the picture suggests a connection to the Masonic third degree, although it could be a reference to the Baphomet.

The Occult Connection

The connection between the Templars, the Freemasons, the Chapel and the occult is rather more difficult to rationalise and its origins are more ephemeral and speculative. One must consider that the entire Chapel was constructed using esoteric principles and proportions enshrined in the 'golden mean', which is, as we shall see, frequently found in the form of many natural objects and equates to a ratio of approx, 1.618. One of the many considerations to be taken into account are the opinions and impressions of several talented psychic mediums who all consider the Chapel to be a unique blend of the physical and spiritual. We shall also discover what happened during the evaluations carried out in the Chapel and see how the mediums are all in agreement about one thing, the existence of a portal between worlds.

Included in a later chapter is the clear implication that there is indeed a link with the forces of 'magic' that, for good or ill, surround us but as we shall see there is perhaps a more appropriate and accurate description of these powers. The area surrounding the Chapel is rich in occult lore stretching back for centuries, and in more recent times the proceedings of the Royal Society of Antiquaries from the 1920's record that two stone-lined chambers were found, one near Borthwick Castle and one near the river at Dalkeith. The chambers were both full of human bones. There is also a recent account from the late 1980's of three tradesmen who visited their place of work at an industrial estate one Sunday night to collect materials for a job the following Monday morning. The estate is located at Loanhead, which is situated between Edinburgh and Rosslyn. The account states that while obtaining the materials from the yard they noticed a figure on the roof of one of the workshops, and at first they assumed it was the security guard.

Abruptly, to their amazement and alarm the figure revealed itself to be not a human being, but some sort of monstrous, wolf-like hominid that leapt from the roof into the yard. Not surprisingly the tradesmen promptly jumped into their truck and made off into the night at high speed. Subsequent investigations revealed no sign of the terrifying visitor and the incident was written off as imagination, well perhaps…but if so why did they all see the same thing? Another recent incident came to light when a walker found another stone-lined chamber close to Borthwick Castle; it too was full of human bones. One must ask if these incidents are related, and if they are, do they have any connection to the Chapel? At any event they do illustrate the strange nature of the locality and its frequent accounts of 'high strangeness' events, and the history of unusual sightings including those of UFOs recorded over the years in the vicinity of the Esk valley on whose edge the Chapel stands.

Lastly we should consider that the Chapel has for many years been a focal point for various groups who seek to harness the sheer latent energy of the place for their own ends; all these requests have all been politely, but firmly, rejected. As we have seen, apart from tourists the only group with regular access to the building, other than the minister and his congregation, are the Militi Templi Scotia, and if there are no Templar connections then there can be little justification for their apparent claim on the Chapel other than a desire to somehow bask in the reflected glory of the reputation of the building.

Enquiries on this matter produced nothing concrete other than the Order have held their ceremonies there for some considerable time and that, other than the *Agnus Dei* (the Lamb of God), carvings of a five-pointed star, a representation of the head of Christ similar to that depicted on the Veil of Veronica, sometimes called 'The Mandylion', and the many depictions of the Croix Patee, there are no symbols within the Chapel that are specifically Templar in nature, although as we have already seen, several of the carvings are dualistic in meaning. It is obvious that Sir William, when he ordered the construction of the Chapel, was well aware that given both the ubiquity and intolerant nature of the Catholic Church he could not include too many details that could in any way be deemed heretical, so he would have been meticulous and circumspect in this matter.

Chapter 6

Rosslyn and the Holy Grail

One of the many claims made for Rosslyn is that, like the stream that runs from Glastonbury Tor in Somerset, England, it is a possible sanctuary for the Holy Grail, although there is no more evidence for this than for the other claims attributed to the Chapel, but still the claim persists, why should this be? Is it perhaps because tradition insists that the Knights Templar, who are inextricably linked to the Chapel, were also alleged to be custodians of this most unique and sacred artefact? It is after all one of the objects that they reputedly sought in the tunnels they excavated below Solomon's Temple in Jerusalem, and immediately prior to their suppression, was supposedly brought out of France along with the contents of their treasuries.

Another reason that the Templars should be seen as the natural custodians of the Grail is because, although the facts tell a different story, they were seen as spiritually pure and therefore the only organisation who could possibly guard such a unique relic; in common with the Arc of the Covenant only the virtuous, pure and Godly could handle it with impunity. First though we should perhaps consider the Holy Grail and what it actually is. Again, although the provenance of the Grail is unclear, tradition holds that it is a cup or goblet, the vessel that was used by Christ at the last supper and later used by Joseph of Arimathea to collect Christ's blood as he ended his life on the cross of Calvary.

Joseph reputedly retained this cup and later brought it with him to Britain when he visited Glastonbury, which was the first major centre of Christianity in Britain, and reputedly the location of the first basic wattle and daub Christian Church. Here he caused the cup, which legend says still contained a bloody residue, to mingle with the stream that runs down from the Tor, thereby imbuing it with healing properties, a belief that still holds true today. Like many holy sites, Glastonbury Abbey was also said to be the repository of several relics, most notably one of the nails from the crucifixion and the milk of the Blessed Virgin Mary. Regarding the existence of Holy Relics, one should be very careful in respect of these artefacts, because in the early Middle Ages there was a extremely lucrative, if macabre, trade in fragments of the saints, and since one bone looks pretty much like another, this created many disputes regarding the provenance of saintly fragments.

Normally this cup is depicted as an elaborate gold receptacle encrusted with gems and pearls, but surely this cannot be true? If Christ truly was the son of a humble carpenter and a man of the people, then he would have used a much more humble drinking vessel befitting his station in life. It was the church he founded that, for reasons of its own, awarded him the cup of a king. It is also a fact that prior to the Council of Nicea in 325AD, Christ was regarded as special but entirely human, but following the deliberations of the Council he became divine. The reasons and politics behind this abrupt change would fill another book on their own so at this time we will not pursue it any further, suffice to say that it is true.

The etymology of the Grail is also slightly confusing since the word 'Grail' comes from the Old French word 'Graal,' which itself is from the Latin word '*Gradalis*' meaning a plate which is used to carry different courses to the table. However, it is the alternative etymology that really sets the cat amongst the pigeons, for here we find '*Sangreal*' for Holy Grail and in Old French '*San Grial*' means Holy Grail and by transposing only one letter we create '*Sang Rial*' meaning Royal Blood and this pun is at the core of the book, *The Holy Blood, and The Holy Grail*, one of the most successful works ever written on the subject of the Grail and its attendant mysteries.

The Holy Grail has, depending on who sought it, taken many forms, and has also been used as a generic term for an ultimate goal or achievement. It is also a term that can be applied to any vessel that produced a never-ending supply of food and drink; a 'Cornucopia' or 'Horn of Plenty'. In the Catholic Church the chalice used to hold communion wafers could even be styled a Grail since, through transubstantiation, it holds the mystical body and blood of Christ. However, the origins of the Grail are rather more general and have roots in both Celtic and Christian traditions. One other symbol for the Grail is a dove and indeed Rosslyn does have such a carving set in the ceiling, a dove with an olive branch in its beak; this, however, does not necessarily confirm that Rosslyn is a Grail Chapel.

There is however yet another possibility regarding this cup, if that is what it is, and this involves a Gnostic group, the Cathars, just before their cruel fate at the conclusion of the lengthy and brutal Albigensian Crusade, which was responsible for the deaths of more than 500,000 poor souls. Such was the bitterness of this crusade, which was authorised by Pope Innocent III in 1209, that it spawned the famous quotation from the papal legate, who, when asked who should be spared the sword, said, "*Kill them all, God will recognise his own*".

The remnants of the Cathar (from the Greek *catharoi*, 'the pure') forces had been besieged from 1243 until 1244 in the lofty fortress of Montsegeur, and finally, in March 1244, the siege was ended with the eventual capitulation of the garrison, although the Crusade itself did not end until 1255. The Cathars had been offered relatively generous terms to end the siege, but such was their conviction in their beliefs that these terms were rejected in favour of voluntary death by burning at the stake. It is reported that some of them climbed voluntarily into the pyres. This tragedy has been likened to the much earlier blockade of Herod's fortress at Massada in the Holy Land, where in AD73, 960 Jewish zealots defied the might of the Roman Tenth Legion. Following the siege, which they could never hope to win, rather than surrender themselves to the Romans the Zealots committed mass suicide by hurling themselves over the sheer cliffs on which Massada was built.

The term, 'Cathar,' could be awarded to anyone holding Gnostic views and the core of Cathar belief considered that there was duality in all things, even God, so that in their view there were two Gods, a non-physical God who was absolutely spiritually pure and another physical manifestation of God, the Rex Mundi or God of the World. This version of God had all the imperfections of the flesh and in the canon of Cathar belief can be likened to Satan. Those at the highest level of Cathar belief, the Perfecti, went as far as adopting a policy of extreme asceticism and celibacy and formally rejecting both Catholicism and their Catholic baptism. Naturally this was viewed as a major heresy and although retribution was not swift it did eventually arrive after the Church felt itself threatened by the sheer number of those holding these beliefs in the Languedoc where the Cathars held sway. Perhaps significantly, some Catholic priests had begun to convert to Catharism and worse still, the Cathars of the Languedoc had refused to pay tithes to the Catholic Church.

The link with the Grail, however tenuous, comes from the belief that, as with stories of the removal of the Templar treasure, prior to the end of the siege four Cathari escaped from the fortress by lowering themselves down the cliff face on ropes carrying with them certain religious artefacts. The nature and destination of these objects is unknown but it must be assumed that they were extremely important to them. The notion of dualism is one of the possible links between Cathar belief, the Grail and Rosslyn. Bear in mind that Sir William Sinclair deliberately packed the building with detailed carvings and imagery, and for reasons of safety and security, there is abundant dualism expressed there.

As with Rosslyn, the Nazis also apparently had an interest in the fortress, this time in the form of SS investigator Otto Rahn, who, as a member of the Ahnenerbe allegedly visited the ruins in 1929. Rahn later produced two popular novels on the Grail legend where he linked the story of Montsegeur and the Cathars to the Grail. As far as the Rahn/Rosslyn connection goes: until 1939 when he resigned from it, Otto Rahn held the rank of Obersturmführer (1st Lieutenant) in the SS and in his role as a kind of Indiana Jones it has been theorised that as part of Himmler's obsessive Grail-quest he arrived in the west of Scotland aboard a German U-Boat, the U33, which it is claimed managed to breach the naval defences and appeared in the River Clyde which runs through the very heart of Glasgow. From here, the story goes, after evaluating some of the Templar sites dotted around the west coast of Scotland he travelled east and ended up in Rosslyn Chapel seeking evidence that the Holy Grail might actually be there. As far as the U33 goes, in 1940 it eventually sank in the waters close to the island of Arran, many of the crew died, but others were captured and interned as POWs. It is also known that either parts of an Enigma code machine, or a possibly one that was complete, was found on board, and this was salvaged and sent to the top secret decoding centre at Bletchley Park to assist in the war effort.

Following years of excavation in the caves, in 1937 Rahn sent Heinrich Himmler a number of objects found during the excavation, one of them was reputedly the Cathars' scared vessel or cup smuggled centuries ago from the fortress above. Himmler was evidently delighted with the booty and had it sited in a place of honour at Wewelsburg castle, the spiritual home of the

SS near Paderborn in Westphalia. The extensive restoration of Wewelsburg was Himmler's obsession and paid for out of SS funding. Because of his fascination with the Templars, Arthurian legend, the Teutonic Knights and the Grail, coupled with his mission to run the SS on similar lines, he regarded the castle as his personal latter day Camelot.

However, Rahn's death two years later has sinister overtones, because on the 13 March 1939, practically on the anniversary of the fall of Montsegeur, Rahn died in the snows of the Tyrolean Mountains; apparently in an act of suicide. While that is perhaps how it was meant to look, it is thought that the very fact that he had by then resigned his commission in the SS was unacceptable, and reason enough to have him killed, and the Gestapo were given the grisly task. The Ahnenerbe (literally ancestral heritage) was created by both Heinrich Himmler and Richard Darré who was also creator of the Nazi "blood and soil" ideology and head of the Race and Settlement Office. Originally founded in 1936, it was eventually fully absorbed into the SS in April 1940, although most of its members were already involved to some degree with the SS.

It was designed to research and prove Himmler's mystical theories concerning the racial origins and superiority of the German people by any means possible; appropriately its headquarters were also at Wewelsburg Castle. One must never lose sight of the fact that the Ahnenerbe was also responsible for many of the ghastly medical experiments carried out in the concentration camps. It is perhaps an unpleasant and unwelcome comparison, but at Wewelsburg, even although its purpose was inherently evil, its construction may have been for the same reasons as those of Rosslyn and there is no doubt that it contained many artefacts held dear (sacred just cannot apply here and defiles the word) to the SS and its wicked ideology. It was, in act if not in deed, the Grail Castle of the Nazi Party, and in particular the SS.

One final possibility for the actual nature of the Grail brings us back once again to the Knights Templar and Rosslyn Chapel; this is the attachment and devotion expressed by the Templars for the Blessed Virgin Mary. While this is one interpretation; if one can accept that in biblical terms there is some ambiguity and confusion between The Virgin Mary and Mary Magdalene, then it is possible that this devotion was actually focused on the Magdalene, but the Catholic Church perverted this in a manner more suited to its own misogynistic paradigm by denouncing her as a fallen woman and a prostitute. In fact there is absolutely no evidence that she was a prostitute, and in these more enlightened days even the Catholic Church will admit this, even though the myth still persists. It is believed that the cult of the Black Madonna, also associated with the Black Isis, Ishtar, Astarte and Lilith, was actively encouraged by the Templars, and that St Bernard of Clairvaux, who was instrumental in creating the order and an uncle of one of its founders, was also a devotee as reputedly were the Cathars.

It has, in addition, through the French punning translation of the San Graal to Sang Rial, (i.e. Blood Royal), been conjectured that this is a reference, not to an inanimate object but a person, in this case Mary Magdalene and the Grail is her womb, the cup or receptacle for Christ's child, the royal blood. This series of examples and comparisons is designed to demonstrate just how flexible the concept of a Grail actually is. We see how by association, if the Templars were associated with the Black Madonna, which is an aspect of the Grail, and the Templars are associated with Rosslyn Chapel where there is a statue of the Madonna and child, then perhaps the Chapel is indeed linked to the Grail. The spider's web of innuendo sends its myriad tendrils into the fabric of history, and binds many apparently disparate strands into a whole.

Part II

The Esoteric Dimension

Chapter 7

The First Evaluation

Note, *This chapter is based on information obtained in 1998, and as such was not written with the benefit of hindsight.*

Because of the continuing speculation regarding Rosslyn and its supposed contents, it seemed appropriate to carry out a survey using the services of clairvoyants who are, from time to time, kind enough to assist in research projects. In this case the mediums were Jim and Anne-Marie Lochhead along with Mairi Tognin, and when I put this suggestion to them to my delight they agreed. To make things more interesting, none of the clairvoyants had been to the Chapel before, and more importantly Jim and his wife had not met Mairi before. The only knowledge that they possessed, like mine, had been gleaned from newspapers and magazines etc, so I was very interested in what they might discover from contact with the building.

We first made contact with the trustees at Rosslyn through Mr. Stewart Beattie, at the time the director of the Rosslyn Project, who looks after the day-to-day logistics of running the Chapel for the trustees. Following some correspondence we were granted permission to visit and see for ourselves what lay there. We set the date for Sunday, May the 16th 1998 at 12 o'clock midday after the regular service had concluded. In the intervening period I had requested a floor plan of the Chapel from Mr. Beattie, which duly arrived. I intended to have one of our clairvoyants examine the plan and try a dowsing technique on it, which, as it transpired, produced a surprising result. When she did this an anomaly was detected at the North East corner of the plan in the 'Lady Chapel'. This anomaly caused the pendulum she was using to oscillate wildly, the medium also had the strong impression of a sword suspended point down in the air above it. The only knowledge I had about this particular area of the Chapel was that a member of the St. Clair family lies interred beneath it

The tomb is clearly marked with a large, engraved, brass plaque set into the floor. On the plan, which dates from the Victorian era, this small area is depicted with dotted lines forming what looks like a union flag. I contacted Mr. Beattie and enquired about this, but he told me that since the book from which the plan had been reproduced had not included an explanation consequently he could not assist us. It has, however, been suggested that what these markings represent is the location of the sculpted arches and cubes in the ceiling above the Chapel floor. It should be noted that although rows of the cubes adorn the ceiling above the entire Lady Chapel, the illustrator may have felt that anything other than a symbolic representation would have obscured too great an area of the floor in the original drawing. Originally the Lady Chapel was supposedly intended as a 'retro choir' for the Chapel and indeed there is some speculation that the entire Chapel may have been intended to serve the same purpose as part of a cathedral. This however, in spite of claims to the contrary, is still a matter of conjecture.

In the days immediately preceding our first visit to the Chapel, one of the mediums, Ann-Marie, was unable to sleep and received a series of images relating to the building, particularly the Lady Chapel. One definite feeling was that (as other people have suspected) sound is an essential part of the puzzle, in particular an odd, high-pitched note, which as we later discovered might be pivotal to unlocking the key to the enigma, not only to the vaults and their alleged contents, but to the Lady Chapel itself and what it actually represents. The medium told me of her suspicions regarding what was there, and if she was correct then this small section of the main Chapel contained a force, an energy that in the right hands had the power for good, or in the wrong hands for a great and profound evil, an impression that, as we will discover, was corroborated some years later in a communication from a lay preacher in the USA. According to the psychic, there are only five of these sites around the world, one is in a Pyramid on the Giza plateau in Egypt, one is in North America, one is high in the Andes Mountains of South America, another is in Africa and now we are told there is one in Rosslyn Chapel. These singular, strange, powerful, potentially dangerous objects are 'Astral Doorways' and its discovery proved to be a unique experience. In light of what was uncovered in the Chapel this 'device', for that in truth is what it is, may have been designed to remove potentially dangerous information from human hands.

My wife Ann, and I, arrived at the Chapel just before mid-day to find two of the mediums, Jim and Anne Marie Lochhead, already waiting outside. We chatted for a few moments until the other psychic, Mairi Tognin, joined us. We identified ourselves to the attendants at the Chapel ticket office then exited into the grounds and entered the beautiful old building just as the congregation was leaving. As the congregation filed out past us we could hear a choir singing quite unaccompanied by any musical instruments. The purity of the voices ringing around the old stones of the church interior was a truly emotional experience and enhanced the powerful feeling of tranquillity and timelessness. In counterpoint to this stillness I have never seen our psychic friends so enthused or energised, it was obvious that the inherent power of the place was already making itself felt.

Chapter 8
Signs and sounds

I decided to follow Jim Lochhead and his wife and record their initial reactions on videotape while Mairi wandered around soaking up the atmosphere. I was concerned that in spite of the beautiful singing, the additional people in the Chapel would have a detrimental effect on the clairvoyants, but fortunately the choir left within about ten minutes of our arrival. Jim and Anne-Marie went to the east end of the Chapel where they sensed the figure of a Templar Knight standing at the wall beside the point where the Astral Doorway had been detected. Significantly, this same feature was found some years later by another medium working only from a photograph I had supplied. The figure appeared to be part of the stonework of the building and once the psychics had drawn my attention to it I could see it quite clearly. This figure was apparently intended to act as a guardian for the Astral Doorway.

The figure was not just a random arrangement of patterns in the stonework, it was clear and well defined and to my surprise, facially it was very reminiscent of the figure on the Turin Shroud. A sudden noise distracted me and I glanced away for a moment and when I looked back again, although I could still see the figure, it slowly faded until it completely disappeared; it looked as if it was being absorbed back into the fabric of the building. I went over to the spot where it had materialised and looked closely at the stonework. I gently ran my fingertips over the surface, but there was no sign of any graining or irregularity that could fool the eye into seeing anything other than a wall. Both of the clairvoyants were obviously aware of a great deal more than I, and of the two Jim was the more engrossed, and seemed to be literally in another world.

Anne-Marie walked over to the left hand corner of the Lady Chapel and paused for a moment then slowly turned in a circle; her eyes were closed. She paused and stood with her back to the altar and crossed her arms over her chest with her eyes still closed. Then she opened her eyes and smiled, obviously pleased with what she had found. I called Jim over to where we stood; I had to call several times as he was deep in thought. He walked over to us and he and his wife discussed her discovery. I experienced a thrill of excitement when I was asked to stand in the area and enter the aura of the energy field. My wife, who had been watching the proceedings came over, I handed her the camcorder to continue taping. I stood in the area vacated by the medium close to the St Matthew altar, extended my arms palms down, closed my eyes and relaxed. Almost immediately I felt something vaguely resilient under my hands and arms as if they were being gently pushed upwards.

The medium said that she would intensify the sensation, and although my eyes were still closed I was briefly aware of her moving her hands over my head. The physical sensation was astonishing; it was like being pushed upwards by a force beneath my heels, it was lifting me from the stone floor. In a matter of seconds I opened my eyes and stumbled forward as if standing on a steep slope, the feeling was quite unique and bizarre. I asked my wife, Ann, if she would like to experience this and she agreed. As she took up position her arms involuntarily rose from her sides and she also felt the sensation of being lifted upwards.

The medium explained what this Astral Doorway was and what it could do, and was at great pains to emphasise its singular nature; when asked to describe it she likened it to a column of white light. The act of spontaneous levitation was as a direct result of the latent energy held in check by the doorway. This extremely rare anomaly provides a 'tunnel' between the physical and the spiritual world, in effect it was a two way street, things go in and perhaps more importantly things come out. Jim, who had been quietly observing, joined in and explained that entire races had gone through doorways like this. According to him the old races had known about these things and although treating them with great reverence and respect, had used them more or less at their will.

Is it possible that race memories of these ancient portals still exist, finding expression in the invention and speculation of sci-fi writers with their matter transmitters and star-gates? Or is there a more acceptable, but still incredible, parallel with current research done on quantum mechanics by theoretical physicists and the possibility of 'worm holes', which are rips in the fabric of the space-time continuum claimed to lead to other galaxies, and as we later discovered this was much closer to the truth than we at first realised. Anne-Marie explained that she could probably open the portal, but she did not think it would be either advisable or safe to do so at this time as the risks outweighed the advantages. Besides, due to possible negative effects to the Chapel, it could only be opened a tiny fraction at a time and even if the existing guardian was willing to permit it, a gatekeeper would still have to be found and left with it to safeguard what was on this side. It is interesting to note that the medium claimed to be able to activate the doorway, which leads to speculation on both the nature of these astonishing artefacts and to the nature of the talent wielded by mediums and psychics. We shall return to this vital matter later in the book.

The American singer
While this all was going on I was surprised to hear loud singing behind me. The source of the singing proved to be a visitor; a large, dark-haired American lady strolling around the Chapel. Quite at random she burst into song; the music was the kind of material frequently performed by Gospel choirs. She was an extremely accomplished singer, but also loud - very, very, loud.

She came over to where we were standing in the Lady Chapel and stood close to the wall with her back to the small, central altar dedicated to the Blessed Virgin Mary. Facing into the choir of the church she burst into song again, nothing complete, just random sections of various gospel songs. At this time the medium was trying to meditate and I assumed that the singing was disturbing her, but it was quite the opposite, the singing had an unexpected result. She opened her eyes and beckoned me across, *"This is how we produce the sound that I heard,"* she said. I asked if she wanted me to ask if the lady would oblige, she nodded in agreement. I asked the singer if she would help and explained what we needed. She seemed at bit bemused at first until I told her of the theory that music, or sound, held the key to unlocking the enigmatic secret of the Chapel, and to our delight she agreed to try.

The medium hesitantly tried to approximate the sound, the American singer listened intently then, closing her eyes she started to alter the tone of her voice while attempting to reproduce the note. We listened as she increased and varied the pitch and volume of her voice, the sound rising and falling in a rhythmic cadence as she sought the correct tone. Her voice reached a plateau of sound and levelled off then she stopped singing, *"How about that, is that what you need?"* she asked. The medium nodded her head saying, *"Can you try again?"* The woman smiled and turned away from us facing back down into the main section of church once again. She opened her mouth and once again the powerful voice reverberated around the building. Her voice rose in pitch until she achieved the note and the whole Chapel came alive and seemed to reverberate, almost resonating in sympathy with the tone; the sound swirled and washed around us.

The sensation is difficult to describe in words, but it felt as if the fabric of the Chapel was becoming as one with the people within it in a strange blend of unity and metamorphosis. Everyone in the building paused to watch what was happening when abruptly she stopped, shook her head and smiled. In the sudden silence there was a faint residual resonance, a humming sound emanating from the very walls and pillars, then slowly the noise faded away to silence and the normal background noises picked up again as people turned away, almost embarrassed. We thanked the woman who left shortly after still singing gospel phrases. Our impression was that we were on the right track, the sound of the woman's voice had, in our opinion, caused an odd resonant humming in the building, a sympathetic frequency. This was a line of investigation I decided to pursue as it tended to corroborate similar lines of inquiry being investigated by other people. At this point I left the clairvoyants and slowly strolled around the Chapel looking at the sheer vibrant complexity of the carvings, with the pagan 'Green Men', blending into the intricate scrollwork and foliage interwoven with flowers and figures.

This building is a genuine masterpiece, a treasury of the masons' art in all its rich variety. I saw Mairi standing in the centre aisle of the Chapel and went across to her; she was obviously still receiving strong impressions from the place. *"The man who built this place was almost a 'Merlin' figure, I can guarantee that he knew exactly what he had here."* She explained that he probably had considerable alchemical and mathematical knowledge, certainly a man who was in tune with the energy of the area. It is speculated that in line with other medieval places of worship, this building was constructed on the ruins of an earlier site of worship, reputedly either a shrine to Mithras or a Druidic temple or perhaps both, but certainly in a timeline stretching back to pre-Christian times. These structures had not been built where they were by accident; none of them, and this area in particular, was a nexus of natural power and a meeting place of many 'Ley-Lines.'

Mairi closed her eyes and stretched out her hands. *"I can see him, standing right here, it's as if he is holding the Ley-Lines like reins, driving this place. This isn't a building in the strict sense, this is a machine, it's like a mechanism"*. She went on, *"This building does not stay still, it moves, it changes with the seasons, it breathes. It doesn't stay totally in this time frame, it's like a fluid"*. *"The treasure isn't anything material, it's the energy and it's here below us in the vaults."* She indicated two stained glass windows set high up near the ceiling. *"These two windows show the changes, if you were to observe them carefully over the year, you would see the seasonal changes. For example, a flower will bloom or a leaf will fall, there will be some small change in the detail."*

I was quite taken aback and felt a thrill of excitement; if anyone would know about this then these talented people would. I have observed this medium on several occasions and had never before seen her as animated and positive as this. Interestingly, years later I heard comments regarding the transitional nature of the building from another source quite unrelated to the medium, but in this case it referred to the carvings that adorn almost every inch of the place. This observer commented that the very carvings on the walls seem to change and alter over the years. Perhaps this is due to the sheer number of decorations and our inability to remember them all, or perhaps the changes are more than merely notional and a spurious demonstration of the life-force imbuing every atom of the structure.

I asked her if she could see anything over in the corner at the Lady Chapel where the astral doorway was located, she smiled, *"Yes, I can see it from here,"* she said. I asked her to describe it. *"It's like a curtain, a shimmering violet curtain, I would like to go over and see if I can pass through it."* This was exciting news and a form of corroboration; one medium saw it as a column of white light while the other perceived it as a shimmering violet curtain. Yes, the perception was different, but the image was still there. This corner was indeed very special, but there was more; anyone getting too close was in danger of 'falling through' into another plane of existence. In the right hand corner Mairi could see another guardian of some kind, this was in the opposite corner from the other figure and he was there to prevent the uninitiated getting too close to the real secret of the Chapel. Not to physically prevent them by force, but instead he would deflect them in some way and stop them seeing the next stage, the next step.

The medium commented that she had been communicating with him, but now that she had noticed the 'doorway', he was ignoring her as if annoyed that she had detected the anomaly. Some years later it later it transpired that this was highly relevant, but the figure seemed to be located at the other side of the Chapel; unless the location of this guardian indicated that part of the secret was hidden in the crypt; something that we found shortly after. As we moved into the Lady Chapel again Anne-Marie, Jim and my wife, Ann, joined us. We stood in the corner clustered around the plaque on the floor marking the last resting place of one of the Sinclair family. Mairi was clearly emotional and becoming quite agitated, and facing the altar she reached out her hands as if about to touch someone, *"I can see their hands reaching for me, they want to come through, I can feel their pain,"* she looked at me. *"There's someone behind you, a guide, wait, there's someone else, Godfearing, strict."*

Unfortunately, I could attach no particular significance to this comment as it could apply to many people, neither was it clear whether this was a family member. However, as we shall discover, this may have been an unwitting reference to the guardian set to watch over and protect this particularly active area within the Chapel. Unfortunately, a number of curious visitors were beginning to gather round and Mairi was becoming visibly upset, so regrettably she 'shut down' and refused to continue. As we shall see, what was sensed at this time was fully corroborated eight years later in even greater detail by another medium working from nothing more than a photograph of the 'doorway'. This new medium also had some surprising things to say about the windows. In fact, as it transpired all of the comments made by the psychics were fully corroborated by the same medium, who had no access whatsoever to any of the revelations made during the earlier investigation. As I already mentioned, this medium worked solely from a photograph supplied by me and he was given no hint whatsoever regarding where the image was taken.

Chapter 9

The Choristers

It was now about three pm and we were in need of a short break, so we retired to the small coffee shop adjacent to the Chapel to relax and discuss what we had seen. Mairi, who had gone outside the building, sensed several structures below the ground, and much to our delight this was later corroborated. She also felt that there should be another door in the south wall and it turned out that there had been, but it had been sealed up many years ago. At this point a reporter from 'The Scotsman' newspaper joined us. He brought a photographer with him, but unfortunately this led to a problem with the Chapel staff who were adamant that since this was for a newspaper there would be no photographs taken without prior consent from their supervisor. Unfortunately, he was not available and no amount of discussion or persuasion would alter their stance, so the net result was that no photographs were taken.

The reporter conducted the interview, which later appeared as a feature in 'The Scotsman'. To be fair, the reporter came with us into the Chapel and Anne-Marie invited him to experience the Astral Doorway, which he did, although without much evident success. He left shortly after this so we went back into the Chapel where we chatted to an new acquaintance, Jim Munro, a guide specialising in specific aspects of the Chapel who was showing a Masonic group around, and indicating some of the Masonic influences. He was very interested in what we were doing and volunteered, once he had finished his tour, to show us some sections of the building that would be of special interest to the clairvoyants. We gratefully accepted and waited for him to finish. As we waited, the sound of singing drifted up from the crypt, so we walked over and carefully descended the worn stairs into the gloom.

There were twenty people, mostly women, in the crypt, standing in the four corners in groups of five. Placed on the floor in the middle of the crypt, which as we have learned predates the Chapel by many years, was a selection of recording equipment, which was in use. We stood in silence enjoying the beauty of the singing which was in a similar vein to a Gregorian chant. The singers were Austrian, and on making enquiries we discovered that they were part of a larger group of people who, on a rota basis, travel to Rosslyn once a month to perform this music. The music is written by a French curate and is intended to be performed solely at Rosslyn. Initially we did not realise what they were doing there, but during a later investigation the likely purpose became clear. It does however serve as another illustration of the magnetic attraction exerted by this small Midlothian shrine. Unfortunately, at that point the singers finished and began packing up their equipment, but we were joined a few moments later by Jim Munro who was keen to show us areas of special interest in the crypt. It has since been speculated that the singers were there attempting to energise the doorway by the use of voice only.

For some reason the singers no longer make the journey to Rosslyn, the sheer expense is one possibility or perhaps it is simply that they were unsuccessful in their endeavours, on the other hand perhaps not and therefore there was no need to return. However, if they were successful no indication of this was sensed by the mediums either then or now. This brings us to the curiously patterned decoration along the apex of the ceiling, the richly engrailed motif used by the Sinclair family and common to all their heraldry. Is it possible that this is not merely decoration, but a deliberate attempt by Sir William to alter the manner in which sound is projected around the enclosed area? In this respect it may have been done for the same reason that the so-called 'relieving chambers' were constructed above the Kings Chamber in the Great Pyramid at Giza. Ostensibly they were designed to take the sheer weight away for this area of the pyramid, but recent research conducted by sonic engineer Tom Danley and others now suggests that they were put there to enhance specific inherent tonal qualities within the pyramid. Can this be direct a parallel with our forefathers, the megalith builders at New Grange and Maeshowe and what Sir William achieved? Remember, not one stone or decoration within this building is there by accident; they are all in their precisely allotted space.

There is a small room set into the north wall of what is referred to as the crypt, which, as we have seen, was used for the storing of plans and sketches during the building of the Chapel. Jim ushered us into the room and closed the door. The room is quite small, little bigger than a large cupboard and there were seven of us so space was restricted. Jim told us that psychics normally felt quite at home here and all of our clairvoyants sensed the presence of great power; Mairi clarified this by saying there was a nexus here beneath us where several ley lines joined. Jim then indicated one of the flagstones and asked that one of us stood there and I quickly complied. He told me to close my eyes, relax and tell him what I could feel. I felt myself begin to gently sway back and forth, the oscillations gradually becoming more pronounced. The flagstone began to feel as if it were moving, undulating beneath my feet and becoming fluid. I opened my eyes and saw one of the mediums standing right in front of me; one of his hands was behind my back the other at my chest in case I fell over.

I was able to recount my impressions to the group and the psychics agreed that this was typical of areas of power such as this. We stood in silence for a few moments absorbing the total tranquillity of the place, then moved back into the crypt again. Jim Munro told us that there were other areas of the Chapel and crypt that produced a similar effect, but not as strongly as the area in the small anteroom. As something of a surprise we noticed the time, which had really zipped by almost unnoticed. Our four hours had passed by in a flash so we made our way out of the Chapel and thanked the staff for their forbearance. In the car park we stood and chatted about the day's events, and one thing that did emerge from our discussions was the conclusion that there is much more information to glean from the building. Whatever Sir William Sinclair's intentions were when he ordered its construction, the Chapel hides its secrets well. There is no easy answer, no 'quick fix', but what we discovered laid the foundations for further research.

Angel, cube and mason's mark

Close up of cube and markings

Close up of portal with light anomaly

Cube close up

Chapter 10
Why Mediums?

The practise of mediumship has been fraught with a mixture of fear, prejudice, speculation and controversy since its informal inception via the Fox sisters in the United States of America during in the 19th century. This was not, of course, when psychic ability began or was known about, but when it assumed a measure of acceptability and perhaps more importantly, respectability. The ability of human beings to contact non-physical entities is probably as old as humankind and was practised in one form or another by tribal shamans. In fact it is likely that the early practitioners of the psychic and divinatory arts were more successful in their endeavours due to a lack of prejudice and preconceptions amongst their intended audience. It was an era when the human race was more in accordance with nature and all that implies, it was also an era when animistic belief was the norm and it was fully accepted that each and every animal and object, organic or inorganic, possessed its unique spiritual attributes.

This being the case there was no reason that in certain circumstances the appointed representatives of the group, tribe or clan could not communicate with the spirit of, for example, a tree, and this is exactly what used to happen before a tree was felled prior to use. Significantly, in parts of Africa it still does. It was also the norm to give thanks to an animal before it was slaughtered for food and clothing and it was important that since the animal had to die that none of it should be wasted; to do otherwise was seen as an affront to its spirit. Since this informal but powerful natural bond existed between human beings and their world, it is no surprise that the practise of ancestor worship should have developed and still remains in some societies.

The cultural taboos forbidding contact with the departed, although basically a fear of the unknown, began with organised religion and the spread of formal monotheism and its demands for an unquestioning belief in a creator God complete with the plethora of rules that entailed. There is much to question in this stance, it is undoubtedly due to self-interest that adherents of any particular belief system seldom query its rules and strictures, preferring that the sole method of contact and communication with the divine remains within the system. However, since the teachings of all religions systems make it clear that after physical death the spirits of the dead move to another state of being, then if one wishes to retain this contact it is only a matter of choice about how this is achieved. The use of mediums or shamans to contact the departed is probably no less valid rather than approved ecclesiastical methods; in modern terms the threats and promises made by the official channels can at best be seen as job protectionism.

The main difference was the quasi-formalisation of the talent and the development of a type of etiquette when dealing with the spirits of the dead. Since those early, heady days of the spiritualist movement when there was a feeling that anything went and there was nothing that was not fair game for the exponents, both legitimate and otherwise, of spiritualism, there has been an inexorable drive for legitimacy and, of course, the ultimate accolade of proof. Unfortunately, the early days of the spiritualist movement revealed that human beings are fallible and this was clearly seen in the number of fraudulent practitioners of spiritualism. This regrettable, but all too human trait, did little to persuade a largely incredulous public to give the concept of contact with their dead relatives any credibility and legitimacy whatsoever. In fact the séance room was a theatrical presentation full of devices and props designed to assist with contact and the medium, in effect, becoming a performer if not the actual ringmaster.

The danger inherent in this type of presentation was the fact that a donation was frequently required to attend these demonstrations of psychic ability and thereby was its potential for abuse. When someone pays money for whatever product or performance, and in this case spirit manifestation was the 'product,' then they are entitled to expect something in return. This of course immediately puts pressure on the medium to deliver the titular product and many did indeed deliver on demand. The problem was that in many cases the mediums resorted to trickery to do so. The wider body of the spiritualist movement did neither themselves, nor the spectacular abilities of genuine mediums, any favours at all by claiming that the fraudulent mediums were 'assisting spirit' to reveal its signs and wonders. This was of course utter nonsense; the only assistance on offer was in pocketing the money of the credulous and gullible.

Although there has always been an air of suspicion surrounding psychics and mediums there are also frissons of apprehension and indeed fear, but these negative emotions are largely undeserved, particularly when the mediums are utterly genuine and open about their talents. The negativity arises because the public perception of mediumship is somehow equated with the perceived darker side of psychic talent, i.e. magic and witchcraft. While this is not necessarily the case, it is also true to say that those who choose to follow other psychic paths to spiritual fulfilment are also gifted with mediumistic talents. It is probably as well to remember that while there is no 'black' or 'white' magic, there is an eternal and elemental source of power that carries no inherent stigma, it is there to be used by those with the knowledge to do so, and it is the purpose for which it is used that creates the division in perception.

It should also be remembered that the abilities of psychics are not solely confined to communion with the essences of the departed; their talents lie much deeper than this. It has often been suggested that all we say and do is preordained and written out for us in this world and the next, and all of these instructions are recorded in the very fabric of reality. This fabric has been called various things; the Collective Unconscious and the Akashic Records are two of them and it has been assumed in some quarters that genuine mediums can access this library of records and extract information from it. In another analogy, which carries echoes of 'The Matrix' series of films, this store of information has also been likened to a type of universal computer hard drive on which we all exist as self-replicating programmes and the information is part of this programme. In this instance the medium acts like the magnetic scanning device that extracts relevant information from the drive.

However, although there have been many attempts to explain just how mediumistic talents function there is no clear winner, but the most recent contender to emerge from the conventions of psychology is called the *'Bicameral Mind'* In this case a psychologist, Julian Jaynes, invented the term to describe how primitive people were able to communicate directly with their gods by suggesting that the left and right brain functions of these people were less inhibited by external forces and humanity was more inclined to trust its instincts. It should be remembered that by convention the right brain is intuitive and associated with psychic events while the left is concerned with logical processes and acts as a censor and jailer for the right hemisphere. Jayne also made a comparison with the 'voices' heard by modern schizophrenics, but made the difference that our ancestors developed this ability as a totally natural adjunct to every day life. In effect they heard their gods speak to them; it was a coping device that helped them make sense of their environment.

This talent was particularly well developed in tribal shamans and in some categories of religious visionaries and Dr Jaynes suggests that schizophrenics only exhibit the traits of their ancestors. If this is true then it gives food for thought and indicates that in times past, those who were cast out of society as mad because they heard voices may only have been manifesting a natural state of psychic ability. How many people are currently incarcerated in psychiatric hospitals subdued by chemical shackles? Is this a genetic throwback and is the bicameral mind breaking through? While this may not be the case, at least it does help to explain in a tangible and mechanistic sense how psychics and psychic ability functions. It has also been suggested by Dr Jaynes that bicameralism may also be involuntarily exhibited in cases of possession, and in its widest sense the development of religion.

This then is one reason that psychics are invaluable in ferreting out information that might otherwise remain beyond the reach of conventional methods of detection. In the case of historical mysteries and enigmas like Rosslyn Chapel we are dealing with a subject that is mired in its own spiritual constraints and of those who caused the place to be constructed. It is entirely possible that the hidden purpose of its builder has been recorded in the very stones of the building, and it is also likely that, as we shall see, the structure is very much more than the sum of its parts. Conventional history can tell us nothing of this, not even if the message was hidden in the fabric of the building. As we shall see, Sir William Sinclair did, in my opinion, hide the necessary information in the designs carved into the walls of the structure; in other words the key lies hidden in plain sight.

Chapter 11
Secrets and treasure

As we have seen there is a great and profound mystery hidden in Rosslyn Chapel; a secret that has so far remained tantalisingly elusive, and since there is a secret what kind of secret is it? Some say that it comprises a fabulous treasure, allegedly the contents of the Templar Preceptories hastily removed from France immediately prior to their arrest and imprisonment in October, 1309. Others insist that is consists of the lost gospels of Christ appropriated from beneath Solomon's Temple, again by the Knights Templar during their lengthy sojourn in the Holy Lands. Another school of thought argues that it is The Holy Grail, the very cup of Christ that lies hidden beneath the floor of this medieval Chapel. Yet others are sure it consists of the Ark of the Covenant, and there are even those who hold that the mummified head of Christ (or indeed John the Baptist) is there.

However, it does not stop with these astonishing assertions. We are even told that the physical and literal gateway to heaven is hidden in the vaults, which as we discovered in one sense is not too far from the truth and incredibly, there are even supposedly the fragments of a crashed UFO. However, finally another and more likely candidate is the Holy Rood, a fragment of the true cross that carried the agonised and brutalised body of the Christ during his crucifixion on Calvary. However, the one undisputed treasure that was at one point at least in the vicinity of the Chapel was the gold and silver plate (among other items) taken for safe keeping from the Palace of Holyrood House during the many wars and skirmishes between Scotland and England, and placed for safe keeping in Rosslyn Castle. It is arguable that at least part of this hoard was also secreted away in the vaults below the Chapel to distribute the precious items more securely.

So, is this supposed secret worldly or spiritual? The fact of the matter is that no one knows what if any treasure lies secreted far beneath this building. The best bet, however, seems to be some kind of spiritual gnosis, a mystical truth and revelation, but what is it and is it still relevant in the 21st century? This is the vexed question lying at the very core of the puzzle. In this chapter I shall present a hypothesis suggesting that as the mediums indicated, yes, the secret is indeed spiritual and although its meaning, significance and focus may have altered slightly over the intervening centuries, this does not mean that it is any less valid - far from it - and it is only now that, perhaps, we are more inclined to accept its truth although, sadly, there is no guarantee of this because there is still the matter of faith in the literal truth of *The Bible*. The search for the truth both spiritual and temporal is a quest that many have embarked upon but very few have tracked to its source and fewer still have found its ultimate reward. Why this should be is not easy to understand, but perhaps part of the answer lies in the fact that the truth exists both internally and externally and one should know one's self before seeking further enlightenment. In this case the enlightenment may be more then we can accept or understand.

While the symbolism inherent in the Chapel's sumptuous carvings and geometry may have been solely for the personal edification of Sir William Sinclair and his family, as we have seen it is unlikely. Rather, this building was designed and left as a learning tool for posterity, a book constructed in one of the most durable mediums available at the time, stone, and intended for those in future generations who could decode the designs and make use of the knowledge locked into them. It is worth noting that the books produced in the Middle Ages were richly illuminated with flowers and foliage and if Rosslyn was designed as a stone book, then the rich decoration is quite appropriate. The connections between Rosslyn and the Freemasons are inescapable, but with the Knights Templar rather less so.

The symbolism entrained in the carvings and architecture is unmistakable for those who recognise the enigmatic signs. Bearing in mind that William Sinclair, who either was a Templar, or at least had strong Templar sympathies, approved every last detail of the building it is obvious that nothing is there by accident. His search for perfection was such that each carving was first created in wood before being sculpted in stone, then numbered and laid in place. Almost every carving in the Chapel carries its own mason's mark, the unique sign or sigil that identifies its creator to other members of that brotherhood. This is particularly true of the cubes in the ceiling of the Lady Chapel. Furthermore, if one takes the time to examine the carvings, other than the abundant stone vines, they are all different and this was deliberate since the masons employed on the construction were well able to reproduce identical pieces if instructed to do so. Again this demonstrates Sir Williams's clear purpose to create something completely unique.

If the supposed secret lies in arcane references to the geometric proportions of buildings, (the so called 'sacred angles' and 'golden mean') or an insight into the esoteric workings of certain secret societies, then it is difficult to see why this has any relevance now. On the other hand, if the carvings contain deliberately suppressed information that could prove disastrous to today's established faiths, particularly the Christian variants, then we are faced with a real and potentially explosive question of choice. Is it better to let well alone and walk away or 'publish and be damned', which in this case just might be literally true? However, as we shall see, if the latest hypothesis is valid then the secret of Rosslyn may be more accessible and wonderful than one might imagine, in fact it may even be hidden in plain sight. This is particularly relevant in terms of concealment, because as the old adage goes, what better place to hide a pebble than on the beach? If the secret is indeed in the carvings then what better way to conceal them than among a cornucopia of carvings, many of which may already carry hidden messages?

The building itself is redolent with history, even the name; 'Rosslyn' is perhaps significant. According to research conducted by Robert Lomas and Christopher Knight for their book, *The Hiram Key*, the word can be broken into its two syllables, 'Ros' and 'Lyn' which have their roots in the Gaelic, 'Ros'- ancient knowledge and 'Lyn'- down the ages. It can therefore be argued that even the name of the place is telling us what it is, a library carved in stone ciphers; an attempt to impart arcane knowledge in something more durable than paper, knowledge available only to those with the intellect to decode it. Outstanding amongst the many and wonderful carvings are two items deserving particular mention; these are the two previously mentioned exquisitely worked pillars at the east end of the Chapel. This is, however, not the only explanation for the name, another tradition suggests that the name refers to 'Ros' meaning promontory and 'Lyn' (or 'Lin') means stream or waterfall, and both of these references are accurate descriptions of the geographical location of the structure.

The Apprentice Pillar

The most impressive of these, the previously mentioned 'Apprentice Pillar,' is a truly marvellous piece of work, which according to legend was supposedly carved by the apprentice of a craftsman who had gone abroad to inspect a similar pillar prior to commencing the project. Upon his return the tradesman saw the finished work and in a fit of jealousy murdered the apprentice with a blow to the head. This head, complete with its deeply scarred forehead, can be seen in bas-relief just over halfway up the wall in the south west corner of the Chapel. There is also another head in the opposite corner, which is reputed to be the murderous master mason. This particular story, although almost certainly an allegory, is a direct reference to a specific Masonic degree of initiation, which is allegedly interwoven with Templar rituals and beliefs; in fact the two organizations are claimed to be inextricably linked. Indeed some of the higher degrees of Freemasonry specifically deal with certain aspects of the Knights Templar to the extent that, as we have seen, the Freemasons claim ownership of certain Templar traditions and rites.

It is important to note that there are many diverse groups claiming direct lineage from the Knights Templar, but obviously they cannot all be right. Another curious interpretation put on the carvings on the apprentice pillar refers to the twin spirals of foliage that climb around the body of the pillar. It has been claimed that as with the twin serpents that coil around the shaft of the caduceus, they are a representation of the twin strands of DNA that are the very blueprint of organic life; of course this interpretation opens up an entirely different can of worms. Another opinion of the pillar and its decorations suggests that it represents both the Tree of Life, which can be identified with Jesus Christ and also the Yggdrassil, which according to Norse mythology is the World Ash. According to the book *The Head of God* by Keith Laidler, the snake that circles the base of the pillar is the Nidhogg serpent that according to legend fed upon the roots of the World Ash.

However, elaborate pillars and treasure vaults aside, perhaps the single most mysterious aspect of the entire building are the enigmatic 'cubes' located in the ceiling of the Lady Chapel, or retro-choir, which is located at the east end of the Chapel. These cubes, which number in their hundreds, are seen emerging from musical instruments played by angels situated at the top of pillars running along the length of the small retro-choir. The cubes rise in silent tribute to the heavens and each cube carries its own set of delicate carvings on all of the exposed faces, what could these carvings mean? It has been suggested that since they emerge from musical instruments, logically, they must represent musical notes, but how can these odd shapes and patterns have any relationship to conventional musical notation?

Chapter 12
The Lady Chapel

Why might Sir William Sinclair have chosen to hide this information in the form of obscure, abstract lines on small sandstone cubes? Could it have been that he wished to express his disapproval and contempt at the summary and draconian treatment visited upon the Knights Templar in 1309 by the Vatican at the behest of King Philip the Fair of France? It is almost certain that Sinclair was very sympathetic to the Templar cause and must have had strong views on their murderous suppression. Likewise, he may also have been aware of a curious and proscribed series of musical notes called *The Devil's Chord* and its eerie effects, and if he intended to use this knowledge to express his dissatisfaction, how could he conceal it without attracting unwelcome attention? The answer seems to have been in a form of a code created by producing stress patterns using fine sand, thin metal plates and a rosined bow of some type. Did Sir William painstakingly create the patterns using this method, transcribing each pattern revealed in the sand onto the stone cubes? We shall return to this important theory later.

The Lady Chapel also contains a bas-relief representation of an angel suspended upside down; this is often assumed to be Lucifer, but is more likely to represent Shemhazai marooned between Heaven and Hell. Like Satan (Azazel), Shemhazai was also one of the fallen angels and one of the so-called 'Watchers' who taught humankind the forbidden arts of chemistry, astronomy, metallurgy, pharmacology and astrology amongst other things. Perhaps Sir William Sinclair, the builder of Rosslyn, had a sense of humour and deliberately depicted the fallen angel descending to hell while his angelic 'music' soared heavenward in a mocking tribute. Additionally, he probably had access to Templar knowledge of Arab occult traditions, which introduces Sufi mystical influences. It is also likely that through the Templars he had access to other mystery schools and their methods of spiritual enlightenment. Perhaps, like Leonardo da Vinci, to save persecution by the Church he hid his acts of rebellion and defiance by encoding oblique references to them into his work as befits the dualism expressed throughout the building.

Before leaving this chapter it is worth noting that in common with what I believe the secret of Rosslyn to be, the story of 'The Watchers' may have more specific relevance to Rosslyn other than a footnote in the books of *The Bible*. Much of what is known of The Watchers and their offspring is told in apocryphal works such as the 'Book of Enoch', therefore what follows much of necessity be taken in that context. We are told that The Watchers, sometimes also called the 'Bene ha Elohim' and 'The Grigori', are the fallen angels, the entities who were among the most favoured of God before they rebelled against him when he decided to award his creations, human beings, a soul. This interpretation tells us that Azazel, who is traditionally identified with Satan and was supposedly one of the powerful angelic Cherubim, refused to bow down before the first human, Adam, and in doing so precipitated the war in heaven that resulted in the eventual expulsion of himself and his followers. Why are they called The Watchers? Because one of the earliest translated accounts of the fallen angels describes them as 'Those who watch', or 'The ones who never sleep'.

It is also insinuated that the fallen angels serve as the original template for demons, the powerful and evil denizens of Hell. This is in itself is another conundrum because in the Greek, '*daimonion*', from which the word demon derives, equates to 'gods' and can also refer to teachers. This is interesting since the fallen angels appear to have acted in this very role and allegedly taught humankind various technical arts including astronomy, metallurgy, medicine and chemistry. The variation in names quite understandably produces much confusion when identifying the fallen angels so, for clarity and for reasons that will shortly become obvious, we shall refer to them exclusively as The Grigori.

We are told that when The Grigori were cast out of heaven, they descended to Earth and cohabited with human women and in doing so produced a mutant, half-breed race called the Nephilim. This race was by all accounts a race of giants and it has even been suggested that the biblical Goliath of Gath, who was slain by David, was one of them. The account of angels interbreeding with human beings must have caused the early church fathers considerable cause for concern because angels were supposed to be non-physical entities composed entirely of spirit, and therefore incapable of any possible sins of the flesh; in this case the use of the word 'spirit' must be a metaphor for energy. How then could non-physical entities cohabit with human beings? This problem is solved by inferring that The Grigori were in some way more akin to human beings (with all their faults) than the enigmatic, altruistic and non-physical angels. It also appears to be a clear nod to the Cathar belief in a physical version of spiritual entities including God, the Rex Mundi.

The half-breed Nephilim were both unruly and aggressive and eventually resorted to cannibalism, at which point almighty God decided to remove them from the face of the Earth. In order to do this he unleashed the mighty Seraphim, the most powerful order among the angelic hierarchy upon them. However, another tradition suggests that the Nephilim were a poor, deformed and sickly breed who were rendered inadequate by the fusion of incompatible genes. In this account God in his mercy sent the Seraphim (also called 'The Shining Ones'), to kill them, which they did and the unfortunate Nephilim were left with their eyes burned out having gazed upon the power and majesty of their angelic killers. So, what then of Shemhazai mentioned at the beginning of the chapter? We are told that he was so appalled when he saw the destruction of his offspring, the Nephilim, that he voluntarily flew into the constellation of Orion where he can still be seen hanging upside down, exactly as he is depicted in the Lady Chapel.

Chapter 13
The Devil's Chord

Is the answer to the enigmatic puzzle music, i.e. sound and therefore frequency? Is this the key to what might or might not be hidden there, and if it is, does it make reference to musical notation that came to be called 'The Devil's Chord'? In the 12th century the Catholic Church gave the musical tone known as the augmented fourth, from C# to F#, the rather sinister title of 'The Devil's Chord' or *'diaboles in musica'*. Also called a tritone, it is an augmented fourth interval consisting of F natural and the B natural above it, it was banned throughout Christendom and this ban, by extension, covered all contemporary European music, whether secular or otherwise. One must ask why the Church imposed this measure, what possible justification might there have been for this extreme sanction? We will return to the subject of The Devil's Chord in more detail shortly.

Was it perhaps because the Church was well aware that this chord, due to its frequency and harmonics, if produced in the correct setting could induce visions and altered states of consciousness in those present, and therefore permit them inadvertent to access the 'divine'? Such an effect would have been anathema to them because it reduced their absolute control over every aspect of the lives of the population; a situation that they would not, and perhaps dared not, tolerate. Or perhaps it acted in the genuine belief that such an effect was the work of Satan and the faithful had to be protected from it at all costs? Whatever the reason, in one way or another it was about maintaining the status quo. This, sadly, was the situation that existed when the Church and State were virtually one and interlinked at all levels. Interestingly it is also claimed that one of the notes, F#, is both the natural harmonic of the planet and the internal resonant frequency of the Great Pyramid. Perhaps significantly it is the pitch to which shamans still tune their flutes.

The Solfeggio Frequencies
Before leaving this section it is perhaps appropriate to consider yet another set of frequencies that, presumably, were sanctioned by the Church and these are the Solfeggio Frequencies. Originally these frequencies were apparently incorporated into official Church music e.g. Gregorian Chants, such as the hymn to St. John the Baptist. However, Catholic Church authorities when asked were rather non-committal about this, claiming that, along with other

styles of sacred music, they were either lost or fell into disuse centuries ago. It is believed that the Solfeggio Frequencies were deliberately harnessed to imbue both those singing them and those listening with feelings of tremendous spiritual awareness when sung in harmony during religious ceremonies. Research into Book of Numbers, Chapter 7 verses 12–83, conducted by one Dr. Joseph Puleo a naturopathic physician, has revealed that there were six base tones or frequencies. This information was extracted using a form of Gematria, an ancient technique for obtaining hidden information by transposing letters into numbers. According to Dr. Puleo the six Solfeggio frequencies include:

UT – 396 Hz – Liberating Guilt and Fear
RE – 417 Hz – Undoing Situations and Facilitating Change
MI – 528 Hz – Transformation and Miracles
FA – 639 Hz – Connecting/Relationships
SOL – 741 Hz – Awakening Intuition
LA – 852 Hz – Returning to Spiritual Order

It is interesting to note that the third note at 528 Hz relates to the note MI on the tonic scale and derives from the phrase '*Mi-ra gestorum*' in Latin meaning 'miracle.' Incredibly, this is also the frequency used by genetic biochemists to manipulate and repair broken DNA strands, i.e. the genetic blueprint upon which life is based. While this is fascinating and apparently corroborating information, it should be viewed with some care.

Although the effects of sound, both positive and negative, are now much better understood this was not always so. The effect that music, which is of course entirely derived from different frequencies of sound, has on human beings is still not particularly well known. It has been used for millennia as an adjunct to meditative states by various mystical groups, e.g. Cabbalists and Sufis, but less so by mystical Christian groups like the Cathars because of their ruthless and systematic suppression by the early Catholic Church. It is also a common technique used by Shamans when inducing altered states of consciousness for magical purposes. Archaeologists have discovered that megalithic structures such as Newgrange in Northern Island and Maeshowe in Orkney appear to have been deliberately constructed to exploit this effect. In the case of Newgrange, which was constructed approx 3,500 years ago, a standing wave of 110Hz has been measured in its long entrance passageway. It has even been suggested that some sets of standing stones were erected to reflect sound from the faces of the monoliths which would act like primitive amplifiers, although the effects would have been much more subtle. If the secret is in fact hidden in the cubes, perhaps we should look at the science behind them.

Chladni Patterns

In an effort to create a visible representation of sound the late Ernst Chladni (1756-1827), a German physicist and father of the science of acoustics, succeeded in producing a variety of patterns representing various frequencies of sound using fine sand, thin metal plates and a violin or cello bow. He used the bow to stroke the edges of the thin metal plates, which were lightly covered in fine sand, then observed and accurately copied down the delicate patterns that formed. He discovered that different frequencies formed a variety of patterns depending on the size and shape of the plate. Crucially, this method of producing sound patterns would have been available to William Sinclair.

Nowadays these experiments are part and parcel of the methods employed in university laboratories to teach the science of acoustics, and although oscillators and vibrating platforms have now replaced the primitive bow and metal plates, the results are virtually identical. The only differences being in the range and consistency of frequencies available using modern technology and when the patterns produced in laboratories are compared with those existing on the cubes there are clear similarities. The only consideration is did Sir William Sinclair actually use this knowledge to encode the information on the stone cubes?

Since many of the patterns on the cubes are almost an exact match for the laboratory produced Chladni Patterns, there is every reason to assume that he did. It has to be made clear that the reproduction of the patterns on the 'cubes' is entirely dependent on having the correct shape of vibrating plates, because plates of differing shapes produce a variety of patterns depending on how and where they are 'bowed'. It would also be vital that whoever was producing the patterns would require advance knowledge of precisely what note they were trying to produce. I should make it abundantly clear that this idea has been floated for some years now and most recently by a hotelier, the late Steven Prior, who employed the services of a musicologist, a computer programmer and a photographer in an attempt to make sense of the carvings. It is not clear if the project was ever completed.

There have been reports that a composer and musician, Mr Stuart Mitchell, decoded the cubes into what he styles as 'cadences', developing and composing a piece of music called *The Rosslyn Motet*. It is difficult to fully understand just how he achieved this since some of the cubes are missing, but in spite of this he claims success. Interestingly, he too discovered the presence of The Devil's Chord. He also asserts that the cubes are cunningly designed to throw the unwary off the scent and included traps and deliberate false trails, so presumably this must include the missing cubes, even though the missing cubes were broken off long after the Chapel was built, probably due to the predations of the Protestant mob during The Reformation. *The Rosslyn Motet* was eventually released on DVD and sounds remarkably like many other examples of medieval music.

If in fact this is the secret of the cubes, can these notes still be reproduced? The answer is almost certainly yes, but to reproduce the original frequencies as intended we would perhaps have to look at how instruments were tuned in medieval times; perhaps more specifically we would need to learn how middle-eastern musical instruments were tuned and reproduce this tuning. As previously mentioned, the Templars had formed a relationship with their Saracen foes based on mutual respect forged in battle. This being the case it is almost certain that given the spiritual core of Templar philosophy, they became privy to certain esoteric practises and customs of Islamic mystical groups, and this would almost certainly include music.

Current musical tunings are based on an 'equal temperament' system, which was not prevalent in medieval times, and therefore any attempt at reproducing the musical notes carved in the stone patterns would have to take this into account. This is not to say that they cannot be reproduced because they can, it has been suggested that the first two notes of the song, 'Maria,' from *West Side Story* reproduce The Devil's Chord or a very close approximation of it, as indeed does the rock classic *Hey Joe* by Jimi Hendrix, plus a number of other musical scores designed to heighten tension in the intended audience. The chord, or tritone, does not appear on any modern guitar, piano or other contemporary instrument, it is however present in certain Mesopotamian tunings, which, once again, introduces a Middle Eastern element.

Over a period of several years many of the mediums and psychics who have visited Rosslyn Chapel are convinced that the answer to the puzzle is indeed musical, or at least directly related to frequency, which, of course is the framework that carries reality. It is interesting to note that during the original evaluation carried out by this author in 1998, as mentioned there was a group of singers in the crypt performing some beautiful, unaccompanied music with the specific purpose of being sung in Rosslyn Chapel. Is it possible that its creator is also attempting to unlock the sonic puzzle of the Chapel?

The following fascinating piece of information comes from a fellow researcher, Mr. Bill Downie, who is amongst other things, a musician. Bill applied the ancient, esoteric, divinatory art of Gematria to the notes that comprise The Devil's Chord and discovered the following information. Significantly, from the information available in this instance Bill defines The Devil's Chord as the notes F#, C & A where, F# = 370 Hz, C = 523Hz and A = 880Hz. On examining these frequencies Bill concluded that they are very close to the following numbers, 373, 515 & 888 and in Gematria we find that 373 literally means 'word' in Greek, 515 (absolute) means Jesus, and 888 means Iesous, which translates to Jesus in Greek. The slight variation in frequency would make little or no difference to how it was perceived by the human ear. However it would be interesting to see the effects on an audience if each frequency was produced using electronic equipment to recreate the frequency of the individual notes comprising The Devil's Chord and also substituting the numerical values of the words for a frequency. There is one final detail to add to the puzzle, as we have seen a few of the cubes are missing and according to the Chapel management their whereabouts is currently unknown.

Does this mean that even if the carvings on the hundreds of other cubes were decoded and transcribed as music with all the appropriate tunings, that the missing cubes would prevent the completed work from being performed? If this is the case then perhaps the final solution is concealed in a few, small, engraved fragment of stone, which are in turn the lost keys to a greater understanding. On the other hand perhaps it is not necessary to perform the entire piece; it may be sufficient to reproduce the frequencies alone to achieve the desired effect. In the end we are all creatures of frequency in one way or another, and as such it is highly likely that specific frequencies can and do interact with human consciousness at some level. If this information is what is encoded in the 'cubes' then it is valid, and at the time when it was put there, a secret with huge implications for the medieval Catholic Church. It would be genuinely fascinating to decode the patterns and finally listen to the music put there by the builder of Rosslyn, frozen in stone for centuries awaiting an intellect that could unlock it.

Chapter 14
The Third Revelation

Events tend to happen in threes, or so we are told, unfortunately for the most part these events tend to be involved with bad tidings for someone; happily, in this instance this was not the case and what was revealed during this short project was experienced by most of those present in Rosslyn Chapel at the time. In this instance the number three in the chapter title refers to what is perhaps the final dénouement in a series of events covering a ten-year period. As we discovered, the first event occurred in 1998 during an evaluation of the Chapel involving the services of four talented mediums. During the evaluation it became abundantly clear that there was a focus here for a range of phenomena not normally encountered in everyday life. Among the range of impressions sensed by the mediums was the feeling that the Chapel was not temporally stable and a very small part of the structure existed in some bizarre, timeless 'otherworld'. Astonishingly, there was also an apparent access portal leading into realms co-existing alongside our own, it was this portal that proved pivotal in the current project.

The second event happened just a few weeks prior to the investigation in September 2005, when an insight was gained into the function of the myriad ornate stone cubes that decorate the roof of the Lady Chapel. Although it had long been assumed that the cubes represented musical notation there was (and is) no consensus regarding its nature. Likewise it had always been assumed that if the cubes did indeed represent music then to unlock any possible secret, it was vital that the piece be played in its entirety. The second revelation came when it became clear that other than an interesting scholarly exercise, rendering the entire musical piece was relatively unimportant, but crucially, its component chords were.

The basic premise came from the reasonable assumption that the builder of Rosslyn Chapel, Sir William Sinclair, may have had an axe to grind with the Catholic Church because of its appalling treatment of the Knights Templar in the years between 1307 and 1314 when Jacques de Molay, the last grand master of the order, was burned at the stake in Paris. The Knights Templar was an organisation with which the Sinclair family almost certainly had strong sympathies and ties, and during the construction phase of the Chapel, Sir William may have registered his disapproval by encoding the notation that defines the previously mentioned Devils Chord (or interval), into the fabric of the building. Sometimes called an augmented fourth, which as we have already seen was utterly proscribed by the Roman Catholic Church in the 12th century for reasons that are still not totally clear, it is assumed that those who played, sang, or listened to the chord were somehow affected by it, probably by achieving an alerted state of consciousness. It is now a simple task to recreate the frequencies that comprise The Devil's Chord using a laptop computer and a set of speakers and as we shall see, the results, although not dramatic, were both exciting and entirely unexpected.

It is difficult to talk about Rosslyn Chapel and remain utterly unbiased by, or detached from, the mystique that surrounds the medieval building. The emotional response of those who enter its sheltering bulk is one of wonder and awe and with small wonder; there is a profound sense of tranquillity entrained in the atmosphere of the place. As already noted, it is almost comparable with the feeling of immense spiritual presence experienced in the Church of the Nativity in Bethlehem. Also, as indicated earlier in this account, the project was triggered by the possibility of a code hidden in the elaborate stone carvings that are part and parcel of the Chapel, the code appeared to be musical symbolism frozen into the stone 'cubes' set in the ceiling of the Lady Chapel, which forms the east end of the main Chapel and it is not the first time that churches and cathedrals have been referred to as 'frozen music'. Since it was probable that the symbols represented musical notation, in this case The Devil's Chord, it was only a relatively straightforward matter of obtaining and reproducing the frequencies corresponding to its individual notes.

The group who assembled to test this hypothesis comprised my wife and I, who facilitated and organised the project, Jim and Anne-Marie Lochhead, two talented mediums who were present at the original 1998 evaluation, Bill Downie, a musician and discoverer of hidden messages in the NIV (New International Version) edition of the Christian bible and an expert in the use of the ancient Hebrew divinatory science of Gematria. In addition, there was the late Mr Steven Hodge, a researcher and psychologist, and Mr Robin Budge, a researcher, and the final member of the group was Mr Nathan Surea, an acoustic therapist. The project was arranged for the 18th of October 2005 at 08.30 to allow us (for obvious reasons) uninterrupted access to the Chapel an hour before it opened its doors to paying customers.

As soon as the group assembled inside the building, the test equipment was assembled; this consisted of a laptop computer programmed with a tone generator and a set of external speakers. The first set of tones entered into the computer were The Devil's Chord comprising the frequency equivalents of the notes, C, A and F#, the notes generated by the computer wafted around the ancient stones of the building. One of the mediums, Anne-Marie Lochhead, immediately sensed that the resulting sound was amplifying a feature that had been noticed in the 1998 venture when an 'Astral Doorway' was first located at the St Matthew Altar in the northeast corner of the Lady Chapel. She sensed that the doorway was 'expanding'. Leaving the computer to its own devices, I stood on the area indicated and felt a definite coldness at one particular spot. The coldness was rising from the floor like an icy draught, note that 1) there was no draught and 2) cold air does not rise, it falls.

The anomaly filled a clearly defined area that extended about six feet to one side of its epicentre then swiftly petered out. The psychologist, Steven Hodge, stood in the same area and felt the sensation immediately. In addition, Steven felt that the impression of coldness stayed with him as he moved away from the area and felt concentrated at the left side of his head and face. It is perhaps interesting to comment that at our first meeting a few days prior to this experiment, Mr Nathan Surea explained that the frequencies comprising The Devil's Chord, to quote him directly, *'Open doors'*, although at the time it was not clear if this was meant literally or figuratively. As some of the others entered the small space to experience the drop in temperature, Nathan began 'toning' a series of notes that were complimentary to those issuing from the computer speakers; they wove a delicate tracery of harmony, the natural, warmer sounds of the human voice blending effortlessly with the pure, but synthetic, tones from speakers.

Nathan began walking slowly around the Chapel and descended into the depths of the crypt, and soon we could hear the sound of toning drifting up the stairs. Hearing this, most of the group went downstairs to join him. The mix of natural toning and the pure, slightly clinical notes from the computer began to blend seamlessly into a pleasant and harmonious whole. The odd but exciting thing was that the two single tones began to produce a third tone, which was almost certainly a harmonic induced by the acoustic properties of the building. We also noticed that when Nathan stopped toning, the harmonic did not die away immediately, but persisted for some time until, eventually, it too faded away. This exercise was deliberately repeated several times with an identical effect, which seems to indicate that there is at least one harmonic, and probably more, associated with the building. It is even possible that like many medieval churches and cathedrals, the structure of Rosslyn Chapel is specifically designed to exploit, amplify and enhance the use of sound. Is this a further example of the fine-tuning created by the engrailed decoration in the crypt?

Anne-Marie rejoined us after her visit to the crypt. Her psychic impression was that there was a circle of people down there, 13 men, all standing in the centre of the floor, all wearing hooded robes; one of them wore the distinctive dress of a Knight Templar. They appeared to be conducting some form of ceremony and there was a reference to a king. I asked if these people were ancient or modern, because the *Militi Templi Scotia*, one of the many groups who revere and perpetuate the order of the Knights Templar, still conduct their ceremonies in the Chapel. She explained that the group was ancient but still lingered within the Chapel. Given the chequered and multi-layered background of the building such a meeting is not impossible, as over the years, many quasi-military organisations must have had access to it, particularly in the 15th and 16th centuries.

The project did not uncover any more anomalies, but it was not designed to, and what we did find was astonishing in itself; there were three distinct elements to it.

- The presence of some form of interface, a point of contact with an intangible realm, this had previously been identified on a previous project in the Chapel.
- The peculiar acoustic properties of the Chapel that created additional harmonics and overtones when a set of frequencies was produced using a computer and the human voice.
- The presence of a group of 'spirits' in the crypt. This anomaly has been noted by other groups who have visited the Chapel, for various reasons it is not likely that our mediums would have been aware of this.

Although what we discovered was not a quantum leap in understanding the secrets of the Chapel, it is another piece in the jigsaw. Perhaps the best explanation of what is concealed there is encapsulated in the idea that Rosslyn Chapel is a book written in stone, and the concept that sound is relevant to it comprises but one page.

This particular investigation was prompted by the possibility that, as previously indicated, sound is crucial to uncovering the secret of Rosslyn Chapel, and on the face of it, it is. The original tone recreating The Devil's Chord appeared to induce a response in the already extant doorway in the Lady Chapel. There was the definite impression of intensely cold air rising in a column from the floor in the northeast corner of the Chapel. There was no sign of a draught or other obvious cause for this temperature drop, so it must be classified as 'anomalous'.

The sighting of a circle of cloaked men in the crypt is an entirely subjective impression received by one of the mediums, and by its nature this account is not repeatable or provable and has to be taken at face value. Finally, and on a slightly different note, there is a distinct lack of 'orb' sightings in the Chapel. This is a phenomenon normally found at sites where there are reports of 'spirit' activity. We have been in the Chapel on numerous occasions taking pictures using flash photography and at no time have we ever captured images of orbs, which seems to give lie to the conventional explanation that they are entirely due to dust and moisture particles suspended in the air. Strangely enough, a few months later I received a digital picture of an orb taken in the vicinity of the Lady Chapel, and we will examine the relevance of this in a late chapter.

What follows are four short and succinct versions of what transpired in the Chapel contributed by some of those present; Bill Downie, Steven Hodge, Jim and Anne-Marie Lochhead and Nathan Surea. Bill has an excellent knowledge of the divinatory art of Gematria. Steven is a psychologist who, fortunately, possesses a keen interest in the paranormal and more importantly an open mind, Anne-Marie is a talented psychic who, with her husband Jim, has assisted us on several investigations, and Nathan Surea is a spiritual quester in the best possible sense of the word.

(1) Bill Downie's account

The first tritone interval we played (370/523 Hz) seemed to have the most effect on Rosslyn Chapel. When I first heard Anne Marie say that the astral portal was opening, I was sceptical. However, after she showed me how to detect the portal, I was more convinced of its existence. The principal effect on me was feeling of coldness in my hands, as if the heat was being drawn out of them. The major event for me was when Nathan began intoning at 370 Hz, the lower of the two notes, corresponding interestingly enough to the word 'logos', (pronounced *low-goss,*) inside the crypt. At first I thought that three or four people were humming, so I descended into the crypt to see what was going on. I was astonished to discover that Nathan was the only person producing a noise! Three things about this experiment were especially noteworthy.

There were at least two other audible tones. These were a fifth and a tenth above the note Nathan was humming, producing a perfect major triad, with the third raised by an octave. The notes, therefore, were F sharp (370 Hz), A sharp (932 Hz) and C sharp (554 Hz). Amazingly, the high A sharp is one of the notes I discovered through Gematria! I also noticed a fourth note at one point. If these were overtones, they were much louder than they should have been. Perhaps the acoustics at Rosslyn amplify the overtones. However, the extra notes did not stop at the same time as Nathan! I have no explanation for this. The psychologist, Steven Hodge, and I, heard and commented on this very strange phenomenon.

The other tritones we played seemed to have less effect than the first. The Solfeggio frequencies we played seemed to have little affect either. However, we did not have enough time to fully explore these. I would like to have heard some 'Solfeggio chords' played. My most powerful memory of the experiment was that Rosslyn seemed to respond to the frequency of 370 Hz, corresponding to the Greek word 'logos'. Now, this is the Word, which implies sound or vibration. I find it intriguing that the corresponding frequency had such an effect on the building. My own instincts would be to further investigate 370 Hz, to see what effects it has on Rosslyn, perhaps with a control experiment carried out in a building of similar size. The metaphysician, Stuart Wilde, has commented that the note F sharp has an effect on the barrier between this universe and the inner planes. Could 370 Hz be some kind of key?

(2) Steven Hodge's Account
As we all entered the Chapel I was immediately struck by how ornate the place was, and I'm sure this was the impression of all those who had never visited before. Heavily carved, Rosslyn Chapel is, aside from the mysteries surrounding it, very aesthetic inside. I believe that both the aesthetics and the specific carvings are designed to effect a specific shift in the thinking of the visitor to Rosslyn – and that we all experienced that shift to a degree. In centuries past, visitors would have 'read' the carvings, almost like a book, in a way akin to heraldry.

It would have told them a "story"; and a powerful one at that given the archetypal spiritual nature of the carvings. (It's also worth pointing out that many of the carvings are non-Christian, being part of the old Celtic/Druidic 'faery faith'. It's rather odd that such was allowed in the time of the Chapel's construction…) Psychologists refer to this as 'signals' (what is represented) and 'signifiers' (the thing in itself), and contemporary visitors to Rosslyn like ourselves, being acclimatised to a much different modern culture don't, sadly, have all of the specific knowledge with which to properly 'read the story' of the carvings properly, to our considerable loss. I noticed that the Chapel design impelled us all throughout the entire proceedings to do what it was, I suspect, designed to do – to direct our attention towards the subjective, internal, existential and archetypal world – via "fascination" and "absorption" (a type of hypnosis that is a clear precursor to meditation).

The place is designed, on many levels, for contemplation and devotion, and clearly for chanting, particularly in the downstairs crypt, which would only further heighten the effects of the place on the mind. In many respects the entire Chapel itself is designed to be a 'doorway' to higher planes. But as for the particular "doorway" we investigated, that was a very interesting occurrence indeed and clearly manifest in a very localised physical space that seems very difficult to explain in terms of 'a draft' or a 'cold spot'. This phenomena needs to be further investigated with accurate temperature readings taken. Rosslyn Chapel is a place that you don't want to leave, and once you do, you want to return to it at some point.

The interior, and possibly the exterior of the building, is - in my opinion - designed to have a direct psycho-spiritual effect on people. As well as being a figurative, archetypal map of the psyche, the "Mystery of Rosslyn Chapel" is the mystery. I'm guessing it represents in many of its carvings – the mystery of the soul and its journey towards final Illumination. This 'uplifting effect' manifested in all of us, demonstrated by the friendly meeting of minds that occurred in the cafe after our investigations, even though we were only in the building for about an hour (yet that one hour seems like it lasted much longer). More information about the original (and modern) societal effects of Rosslyn Chapel 'being there' and 'used as a church' together with a qualitative, ethnographic study of the, individual, psycho-spiritual effects of frequenting the building regularly would, in my opinion, complement any quantitative/physical, research of the location in a way that would provide us with a more complete 'narrative' of the "Mystery of Rosslyn Chapel". It's just unfortunate we can't travel back in time and ask the builders!

(3) Jim and Anne-Marie Lochhead's account

We found that there were many things all going on at the same time; the most important was the energy the notes gave the doorway and I did wonder if these notes would continue to vibrate after we left. We found the doorway had expanded almost like something in a *Star Trek* or *Dr Who* episode. We felt the energy as a real thing in existence that only a TV program could find the words to describe, (if you know what I mean). If that is the case then that suggests that someone out there knows a thing or two. (*Authors Note: it has often been speculated that the writers of science fiction stories unknowingly tap into a vast reservoir of knowledge and information inaccessible to the rest of humanity*) We also saw thirteen people downstairs wearing ancient robes; one of them was a [Knight] Templar. I asked what they were doing and they said they were waiting for the king. Many questions have come to us about this. Who is the king? What is his importance? Why did we not get more? Maybe [it was] not the right time.

The notes you played were exactly what we imagined from the things picked up there many years ago. Like a jigsaw it is all coming together. The fact [that] Nathan chanted added [an additional] dimension and that is what it is all about: other dimensions. We felt that everyone would be changed in someway and we still feel tingly since the visit. We also feel that our attitude is changing to become more matter of fact and accepting of that that cannot be seen. For sometimes we have been like you and cannot find a word to describe where we are at with all this. Sprit etc. has not filled the definition of our experiences. We felt that the ladies altar [Lady Chapel] has changed a lot and that there will be some activity taking place there, we would not be surprised if this becomes the next on the list of ghost walks. We feel that some people who visit may experience things they did not to have on their tour. The energy, the coldness, and the people all add up to reveal that something has opened up there, even if not the doorway, then a portal for future events that when reported will astound people.

(4) Nathan Surea's account

My take on it is this – I could feel the presence of the gateway / portal, a definite drop in temperature, tingling on the hands etc – but I was instinctively / intuitively drawn down to the Crypt. The day before, when I had wandered around outside the Chapel – I felt a strong notion that it (the Crypt) would figure in the proceedings, although, at the time, I did not know what that part of the building was! I am very used to Toning and finding the resonant frequency of acoustic spaces. The Crypt was a perfect resonator- one which surpasses all the others I've experienced worldwide. It could be resonated with the softest of tones. What you experience when doing this is that your voice and the surrounding space becomes one.

There appears to be no separation between your note and the resonance of the space. My feelings are that the Crypt was / is a resonant chamber which sets up different frequencies / vibrations in the Chapel itself, hence the appearance of the other harmonics. I'm excited to hear that you all experienced these sounds; I was lost in the harmony of the Crypt and didn't hear them – but I am fully aware of the phenomena, the Chapel obviously resonates in different areas, with different harmonics, when the Crypt is 'tuned' – like the effect of harmonics on a Harp – you pluck one string – and the others will vibrate due to resonance. Please count me in when you do the next experiments! I think we should definitely explore the effects of the human voice and different harmonics in the Chapel/Crypt.

Here we have four distinct and exciting takes on one shared experience, each one reflecting the interests and inclinations of the person making it, but all contain common threads of wonder and enchantment. What Bill implies in the last few words of his account has far reaching implications for the boundaries of consciousness and how we transcend them. It also seems to imply that Rosslyn Chapel, like many ancient buildings, is far more than the sum of its parts. Steven's input is, as one would expect, slightly more clinical and detached and all the more welcome for it. There are undoubtedly some sound psychological reasons why some sacred places and buildings imbue a definite feeling of exhilaration, and in the case of Rosslyn both wonder and tranquillity in those who enter it.

As expected, the account of the two mediums is deeply spiritual and relies entirely on their subjective impressions gained through methods not normally available to the rest of us. It does however appear that in the case of the 'doorway' at least, we were all privileged to share in the power inherent in this very special place. The rest of their observations will hopefully, in time, be proved correct. Nathan, through his healing work, is obviously spiritually aware and more inclined to project and empathise with his environment and his observations regarding the function of the crypt in relation to the Chapel are a mark of this.

It also seems to tie in with what Bill has to say, it is a facet of the exercise that deserves further investigation. One very unusual occurrence that took place while I stood in front of the St Matthew altar concerned the sudden appearance of an anomalous light. I was standing in front of the altar facing into the chapel when one of the mediums abruptly said, *"Something is happening right behind you"*. I turned round to face the altar and simultaneously pressed the shutter release on the digital camera I had with me. I could see nothing unusual, but on looking at the camera screen there was a bright blob of light illuminating the centre of the engrailed cross in the middle of the altar. There were no additional lights and no torches or spotlights in use, neither was the camera flash switched on yet there was a bright, tightly focussed light shining on this small part of the altar. I have no explanation for this other than according to psychics there was a lot of 'energy' (for want of a better word) around at the time, so perhaps this contributed to what occurred.

Unfortunately, for various reasons many of these questions may never be answered, in most cases it is because they defy rationality. It is arguable that phenomena like these are unimportant in the scheme of things and there are many more pressing needs to be addressed before we explore the inner realms of consciousness and magic. While this paradigm has validity we must never lose sight of the fact that human beings, with all their failings and faults, are creatures of spirit and energy. In addition to this we have an inbuilt curiosity to discover all there is to know about the world around us, both visible and invisible, and as long as we maintain this curiosity then eventually the truth will emerge whether we want it to or not.

Finally, although I had originally thought that the musical tunings might have to reflect the era in which the original notes were created, it appears that it did not matter, at least not in any obvious fashion, however there is another possibility here. It may be that the already heightened sensitivities of the mediums can use the available frequencies and unconsciously adapt them using their own talents, but it may be that if the correct tunings are used then the doorway might open spontaneously without any need for any mediumistic help, and depending on the nature of what is hidden there it has the potential for catastrophe.

It is also interesting that in spite of my earlier thoughts about the necessity of reproducing the tones using the appropriate instruments and tunings of the era, this does not seem to have been the case. The specific tones reproduced electronically using a tone generator and a laptop computer apparently succeeded in creating at alteration in perception within the Chapel, in this case the 'doorway' expanded and became much more noticeable. Does this mean that the notes do not matter provided the correct musical interval in created irrespective of what is used in their creation? Is it also possible that using the appropriate instruments might create a subtly different experience? While this may well be the case, the effects found using a modern electronic simulator combined with modern tunings proved quite remarkable, and as we will discover, the effects of these frequencies on another medium was equally astonishing. In this case I recorded the tones on to a CD and sent it to him, he evaluated it on himself and a colleague and the results were remarkable, we look at this shortly.

Chapter 15
Into the Vortex

The ambience of any given building is dependent on many factors and not all of them physical, and in the case of Rosslyn there are other attributes including the highly subjective impression of immense latent power and spirituality. The spirituality could possibly be attributed to the single fact that it is still a functioning place of worship and contemplation, a purpose it has fulfilled one way or another for over six hundred years, but as we have seen there are much deeper underlying reasons for this. It is to be said that the intricate carvings and loving attention to detail are obvious clues to the physical beauty of the structure, but the real reason lies much, much deeper, perhaps in the unconscious but fundamental interaction between the building and its occupants. Does the repeated use of invocation and prayer subtly alter the fabric of the structure and might this be true of all places of worship, and more importantly is this achieved without the need for a God?

The recent influx of visitors to the Chapel has, on a practical level, been a much needed financial boon to the Rosslyn Trustees and all those charged with caring for the welfare of building, but this new found wealth has been a two edged sword. Apart from the obvious physical wear and tear there is another factor of degradation shared with the tomb of the legendary Egyptian boy king Tutankhamen, and that is the long-term effects of condensation created by the moisture contained in human breath. This was demonstrated when the world famous Egyptian tomb was recently closed to the public to rectify the damage caused by this unlikely source, and similar conditions are now being noted in Rosslyn. There are currently plans afoot to limit the numbers of visitors and this may have to be put in place after the release of the film version of 'The Da Vinci Code', the book by Dan Brown that has almost single-handed been responsible for the sudden and disproportionate influx of visitors to the Chapel.

In addition to this unlikely source of erosion there is another even less obvious and infinitely more subtle cause of damage, not to the stonework but to the very essence of the structure. Is it possible that each person who has entered the calming confines of the interior has played their own part by contributing to a subtle and detrimental osmosis that is perhaps destabilising and diminishing the very soul of the building? Can it be possible that by the very act of being inside the Chapel they have in some way unwittingly taken away a minute quantity of the faith, hopes and devotion of pilgrims who travelled to Rosslyn over the centuries, each contributing to the sense tranquillity that permeates the place? Perhaps they have, but its effects are much less immediately obvious. Aside from this there is a genuine fear that any additional dampness will undo the excellent results resulting from the construction of the large canopy that shields the building from the elements. Prior to its construction parts of the Chapel interior were actually tinted green from the growth of lichens caused by dampness seeping down from the roof. This was certainly the case when I first visited the Chapel in the years immediately prior to the initial investigation in 1998.

The Stone Tape Theory

It has been said that stone, particularly sandstone, has a crystalline matrix capable of recording specific emotions like a type of inorganic but sentient interface. It is this alleged property that has from time to time been associated with the appearance of ghostly figures in various so-called haunted locations throughout the world. This is known as the 'stone tape' explanation for hauntings, where various events become lodged in the subatomic structure of any given building or structure to be revealed to a suitably sensitive person in a similar manner to which recordings are made on magnetic tape: they replay. While this theory satisfies many of the parameters necessary to explain the phenomenon of hauntings, it does not explain them all.

One of the best-known examples of this theory concerns the near legendary sightings of a troop of Roman soldiers who were observed by a terrified electrician while he was installing wiring in the cellars of the Treasurers House situated in the ancient English city of York. As the workman went about his task far below the main building he observed soldiers and horses emerge from one passage wall a few feet away, cross the floor and disappear into the opposite wall. His description of the soldiers and their apparel was unusual, but - as it transpired - totally accurate. This sighting has been attributed to ancient images and events locked into the crystalline matrix of the stonework of the passage and surrounding area. Another example of this is in Westminster Abbey in London where a priest is occasionally observed crossing the floor, but at a level of about two inches above it. Crucially, this was the level of the floor centuries ago, so the recording is true to the era. Another example of this is the stagecoach sometimes seen speeding along Bell Lane in Enfield, London. In this instance the stagecoach is approximately six feet above the ground, and again this is in keeping with the ground level of two hundred years ago.

This is where the stone tape theory might not hold true, if the playback of the recorded scene is on a personal level; if it takes place solely in the head of the observer, then there should be no multiple sightings and the analogy of a video-player is false. However, in some cases there are multiple sightings so this opens up another avenue of speculation. Does the sensitive actually, in effect, 'broadcast' the information into the visual cortex of the other witnesses, or does the playback happen simultaneously for all those present? On the other hand, it has been suggested that sandstone (which is abundant in the Chapel) has unique properties based on its composition, and only requires the addition of moisture and electrolytes to potentially create hundreds of thousands of miniscule batteries within its crystalline structure and it is these primitive, 'proto-batteries' that supply the power needed to energise the apparitions seen.

Perhaps the presence of condensation is adding to the formation of these multiple, miniscule electrical sources. This is also true of various areas throughout the country, that are allegedly 'haunted', (Rosslyn itself is underpinned by layers of mudstone and sandstone), but in this case the power comes from beneath the ground and for the same or similar reasons. The release or discharge of the stored power may be caused by naturally occurring micro tremors in the underlying strata and result in the generation of a short lived electrical pulse above ground. It is thought that this pulse may directly affect the brain of sensitive people in the vicinity and induce an altered state of consciousness. It may be this altered state that allows them a glimpse of what we refer to as the 'spirit world'. It is sometimes strange to think that spirit entities are around us most, if not all of the time, however it is only in specific circumstances that we can contact them. Rosslyn Chapel and the nearby Rosslyn Castle, in addition to their other attributes, have their own ghosts. In the case of the Chapel these are reputedly monks and a 'white lady', while the castle has a mounted knight and a red eyed spectral hound, perhaps a variant on the traditional black shuck or black dog of legend. As we have seen, the monks, or at least robed figures, have been detected by various mediums who have visited the Chapel, but as yet there has been no mention of the ubiquitous white lady.

The Ley Lines

There is yet another possible power source for the phenomena present in the Chapel and that is the natural power created by the planet itself, ley lines. These lines that were first described in the early 1930s by Alfred Watkins, and form a web of raw energy that surrounds the world we live on. They are claimed to be the cause of a whole range of paranormal phenomena. In the case of Rosslyn there are several ley lines, one of which allegedly runs from Queensferry, which is about 15 miles from Rosslyn, right through the Chapel and continues south through several cathedrals in France and Spain and right on to Jerusalem in the Holy Land. It also appears that many ancient monuments, stones circles and monoliths etc, also tend to group around the invisible paths as they forge their arrow-straight lines through the countryside.

Some reports even suggest that UFOs appear to follow these paths and use them as beacons and direction indicators; in fact it has even been suggested that Rosslyn Chapel is a node of UFO activity with a complete craft buried below the Chapel. This story is unfortunately very difficult, if not impossible, to prove. It could, however, be argued that the magnetic field of the planet itself might serve as a marker, or that the lines of planetary magnetic force could even serve as a power source for these supposed craft, but once again this is nigh on impossible to verify. If on the other hand there is a powerful ley line running through the area, then it must have predated the existence of the Chapel and it helps to corroborate the theory that the actual site of the Chapel has always been venerated as a place of power, worship and healing.

Subjectively, while undertaking investigations during 2005 in the Chapel, my wife sensed the powerful impression of movement underfoot while standing on a section of the crypt floor.

The sense of movement and feeling of energy in this particular area was not present some years ago and it may be the result of a steady, but inexorable strengthening of the natural forces that converge on the building. It has already been suggested that the Chapel may act as an amplifier and control mechanism for these energies and that there may be a definite purpose for the increase of energy in the area. Perhaps it is connected to the astral doorway within the Chapel, and it is even likely that the secret of the Chapel may not be a secret for too much longer. If, as several mediums have said, the doorway works in both directions, then we may well see some manifestation of what lies on the other side of the portal, or perhaps we will finally see what William Sinclair concealed there.

Chapter 16
The Baphomet

If we can accept that there is an anomaly present in the Chapel, then it is possible that Sir William Sinclair did engineer an impregnable, non-physical doorway within its confines, and if he did then we can logically ask if he used it, not to travel between dimensions, but instead to conceal something, and if so then what might it have been. As we have already seen, Keith Laidler in his meticulously researched book, *The Head of God*, states that the Apprentice Pillar allegedly conceals an amazing artefact, so amazing in fact that at one point the implications arising from its discovery might have utterly destroyed one of the major branches of Christianity, although this is less likely now. This artefact, according to Dr Laidler, is nothing less than the mummified head of Jesus Christ and crucially, it is clearly implied that the enigmatic Baphomet may in fact be this very head and here we enter a theological minefield, but since it is of great relevance to what may or may not have been concealed in the Chapel we should perhaps look at some of the background.

Since one of the central pillars of Catholic belief is that Christ ascended bodily into heaven after his death on Calvary, how could there possibly be any physical trace left on earth? This is why, unlike an embarrassing abundance of saintly relics, there are no physical relics of Christ except allegedly for his foreskin, or prepuce, which was of course removed shortly after his birth as is still the custom with all male Jewish children. However, since it was the custom at that time to bury the prepuce it is unlikely to have survived in any form. It is noted that there have been many claimants for the Holy Prepuce and during the Middle Ages the honour fell to the abbey of Charroux whose monks claimed it had been given to them by Charlemagne. He in turn claimed it had been given to him be an angel, although another version says that it was a wedding gift to him from the Byzantine Empress Irene. Evidently in the 12th century it was taken to Rome where Pope Innocent III was asked to make a ruling on its authenticity, something that he seems not to have done.

Another medieval claimant to its possession was another abbey church, in this case Coulombs in the diocese of Chartres. Other ecclesiastical claimants included the Cathedral of Le Puy-de-Velay, Santiago de Compostella and the city of Antwerp. Of the others there is one that is particularly interesting and that is the village church in Calcata, Italy. Here, as recently as

1983, they took the relic though he streets in procession to mark the Feast of the Circumcision, a practise formerly authorised by the Catholic Church. However, following the Vatican II council, the practise of venerating relics has, in general, markedly declined with the belief in the miraculous properties of relics being downgraded to 'pious legend'. It is probably best not to dwell too long on the 17th century observations of the scholar and theologian, Leo Allatius, who offered the interesting possibility that the Holy Prepuce may have ascended to heaven at the same time as Christ and transformed itself into the rings of Saturn.

Belief in the existence and efficacy of another relic, the Holy Umbilical Cord, which was likewise originally a Christly relic of the first order, has for the same reasons declined. It is also reasonable to point out that some cures may well have been occasioned by exposure to holy relics, however this may have been less to do with the relic itself and more about the state of mind of the affected person. There have been several documented accounts of spontaneous remission in people who believe themselves to be cured of some medical ailment. This phenomenon is also found in those who believe in the efficacy of prayer and considerable time has been spent in validating these beliefs. The closest one can come to scientific proof of wishing (or praying for) something to happen is in 'The Observer Effect', a peculiarity found in quantum physics that states that nothing can exist until it is observed. The implication here is that something can be wished into being or an event to occur which is exactly what happens with prayer, and in this case miraculous relics.

What then of Christ's head? Although still astonishing, this idea has a more solid basis for belief, since, if the confession extracted from the Knights Templar following their suppression in 1307 is to be believed, they, amongst other heresies, worshiped a pagan, possibly demonic object, a head known as the Baphomet. The downfall of the Templars is intimately connected with the Sinclair family, and as we have seen, in particular with Sir William Sinclair, it may after all have been the reason why he hid the key to what may be the ultimate heresy in the fabric of the shrine he designed and paid for. If indeed the Templars did pay homage to something called the Baphomet, we should perhaps examine this strange artefact in some detail.

The Baphomet appears in various guises; in some accounts it is a head and in others it is a Satanic, hermaphrodite goat. The goat interpretation was eagerly embraced by a number of occultists, most notably Alphonse Louis Constant, better known as the mage Eliphas Levi, and Aleister Crowley, and more recently by, amongst others, Anton Szandor La Vey, founder and high priest of The Church of Satan. In this incarnation, especially in connection with Levi, it is sometimes referred to as the Goat of Mendes. Levi gives the following description of the Baphomet/goat:

- The head of a goat,
- The upper body of a woman
- Cloven feet
- A pair of wings
- A candle on its head
- A symbol of revelation combining male potency and the four elements and intelligence

Although this image gained popular acceptance in the public psyche, due to its passing similarity with the gargoyles found on the roof of Templar Preceptories it is not necessarily accurate. The nearest contemporary image depicting the Sabbatic Goat of Mendes is found in a painting by Francisco Goya, who, in 1800, painted *The Witches Sabbat* which shows a group of women offering their children to a seated goat. Yet another variant on the word, Baphomet, suggests that it can be interpreted as meaning 'Sophia' the Greek word for wisdom. This certainly appears to corroborate two alternate interpretations. Levi's stated that Baphomet is comprised of the abbreviations 'Temp Ohp Ab' that are rooted in the Latin, *Templi omnium hominum pacis abhas* meaning 'The father of universal peace among men'. On the other hand the word may originate from the Arabic 'Abu-fihamat', or 'father of understanding'. Finally, Anton La Vey and his Church of Satan claimed that 'Baphomet' was their identifying symbol normally surrounded by five Hebrew letters spelling LNYThN or 'Leviathan', one of the Lords of Hell. On the other hand, alternative reports of this object describe it as either a skull, or having skull-like qualities, and having the feeling of smoothness, or yet again as having a beard. Of all the available descriptions, the reference to a head seem the more credible and is supported to some extent by the confessions extracted from the captured Templars.

Why should any of these attributes have any relevance to the Templars? There are a number of theories; the most easily discredited is based on the curious relationship that developed between the Templars and their adversaries, the Assassins, during the Crusades. The relationship was founded on the mutual respect that sometimes develops between highly skilled and courageous warriors. We should not forget that in this era there was considerable honour and chivalry shown between combatants, and in spite of the fact that they would still hack one another to pieces should it prove necessary, they also respected selfless courage and valour. Due to this relationship a degree of tolerance and friendship based on mutual respect developed between the two sides and it is possible that the Templars gradually absorbed some traits of Islamic mystical belief and, therefore, it is speculated that 'Baphomet' is a corruption of Mohammed or 'Mahomet'. In fact great care should be taken before ascribing non-Arabic translations to Arabic words, because the Arabic language frequently employs phonetic interpretations when expressing words in written form, and these can obviously vary.

Other schools of thought argue that this is unlikely since Muslims have absolutely no truck with idolatry in any form, although there is no reason that the Templars may not have been pragmatic enough to adapt the name to suit. Another explanation is one that again introduces the idea of knowledge; this one offers the explanation that Baphomet is the amalgamation of two Greek words meaning absorption into wisdom. Whatever the truth, the fact still remains that the Templars confessed (admittedly under extreme duress) to paying homage to, and conducting rituals in front of, the image of an entity called Baphomet. Since we have this connection and there is some evidence that it may be concealed in Rosslyn Chapel, it is possible that Sir William Sinclair, in the sincere belief that it possessed great power and to prevent it falling into profane hands , caused it to be taken through the doorway.

As mentioned elsewhere in this book, the other possibility is that the head, if indeed there is a head, is that of St John the Baptist and since St John was beheaded, once again we encounter the idea of the head, but without the need to contemplate the decapitation of Christ. This is relevant because there is a Gnostic school of thought that believes the Baptist was at least equal to Christ in many respects. In fact the Cathar heresy, among other things, believed that John the Baptist was a demon while the Johanite heresy postulates that John the Baptist was Christ. It is far from obvious whether either belief system contradicts the other, since the Cathars originated from the Bogomil tradition, which in turn accepted and practised a version of the Johanite Heresy. As we have seen, the dualistic nature of Gnostic belief systems like the unfortunate Cathars held that there were two gods, a spiritual God and the 'Rex Mundi', or God of the world. This belief system led to the brutal and systematic oppression and murder of the Cathars by the Catholic Church.

From the occult perspective, in former times it was a commonly accepted belief in that in order to obtain real power one had to either subdue or dominate the spirit of a demon or a murdered man. In the case of the murdered man the seat of the soul, and therefore power, was, during life, supposedly in the head. More worryingly, once again in occult circles, it is claimed that whoever possesses the head of the Baptist will rule the world. This being the case, if the head was that of the Baptist then it scores highly in all categories, and if, as has been speculated, Sir William and his descendents were students and practitioners of high magic, then the significance becomes obvious. While still on the subject of mysterious heads, it has also been suggested that the Baphomet may in fact be the notorious Mitchell-Hedges 'crystal skull', an intricately carved, life-sized representation of a human skull allegedly taken from a Mayan city in Honduras in 1927 during an archaeological dig. Whether or not this is true is open to conjecture, but the artifact reputedly has some genuinely eerie properties. There is another story that it was brought back from the Holy Land by the Templars and kept by them at the Inner Sanctum in London from where, over time, it eventually drifted into the antiques market. One other interpretation of the Baphomet suggests that it was the head of the first Templar Grand Master, *'who made us and has not left us'*.

Part Three

On the Other Side

Chapter 17
Stargate Rosslyn?

It is at this point we must take a step even further out and examine a prospect that seems at first sight to be utterly impossible: that the Chapel might have literal and genuine, non-spiritual, otherworldly connotations. It is the possibility that the Chapel forms part of a larger device designed to act as both a beacon and means of travelling between galaxies; a Stargate, the artefact that was touched upon during the first visit in 1998. Certainly there are a disproportionately large number of UFO sightings in the vicinity of Rosslyn Chapel, which appears to indicate that there is something special about the area. Although instinctively we might initially feel repulsed by such a notion, it is worth examining.

On a more sinister level it might even be possible that persons unknown from this side are deliberately orchestrating a change in an attempt to prize the astral doorway open for unknown purposes. The worrying factor here is exactly who might be attempting to open the door and more importantly why? It is now that we must confront one of the strangest purposes for this doorway, that of an inter-dimensional gateway to an alternate universe. Even stranger, perhaps the doorway is but one of many doorways in the multiverse. Could the incredible astral doorway be, in effect, a Stargate? At first glance this seems impossible, how can there be a Stargate? These artefacts are the very stuff of science fiction, the staple fare of television and cinema, or are they? In 1935, the physicist, Albert Einstein, in collaboration with a colleague Nathan Rosen, calculated that black holes are connected with what they termed a 'throat' connecting one black hole to another black hole. It was eventually called the 'Einstein-Rosen Bridge'; this is effectively a Stargate connecting two galaxies, what we are discussing here may effectively be the same thing, but, using a vastly different technology, the only differences are in the scale and context.

Are there any other possible non-human or extraterrestrial connections here? Perhaps there are, this time not directly through the Sinclairs, but through another group mentioned earlier in the book; the Merovingian Dynasty of France. According to the stories and legends surrounding this French Royal House, the founder of the dynasty, Merovee, was fathered by a strange being called the Quinotaur. The legend goes on to say that his mother who was already with child by her husband, King Clodio, was attacked and impregnated by a scaled, half-human being while swimming and the resulting child was called Merovee. This of course adds a whole new dimension to the story involving an entirely new evolutionary stream of reptile/human crossbreeds, but it might also hint at the evolutionary path taken by human beings since their aquatic origins.

If one can accept that contact with the realm of spirit and demonstrations of channelling, which involves an incredibly subtle but human talent, is in reality a demonstration of a type of technology, then why can what is concealed in Rosslyn not also be a demonstration of an allied technology? It is here that we must consider the theory that Rosslyn Chapel stands on a maze of tunnels and cavities, both natural and artificial, and within the complex is located a genuinely unearthly device of truly supernatural potential. It is regrettable that the videotape showing my brief and involuntary instance of levitation made during the initial visit to the Chapel was loaned to a major television company and unfortunately was never returned, and repeated requests to do so had no effect.

This was inconvenient and on its own might have been dismissed as nothing more than an annoying coincidence, however in the light of what happened when, in 2005, I contributed to a television programme on the phenomena surrounding Rosslyn Chapel and my contribution was, regrettably, totally misrepresented, this amounted to an attack on my own credibility and that of two of the mediums who appeared in the programme and by inference to what we revealed during our investigation. While this once again might have been another coincidence, it does appear that it might also be a clumsy attempt to discredit a valuable contribution designed to clarify the hidden purpose of the Chapel. If this is indeed the case, one must ask why, and on whose behalf?

Chapter 18
What Lies Below?

From what we have already seen there appears to be a legacy of strange powers and legends attached to both the Chapel and the area, but where can this possibly come from? Perhaps we should consider not the Chapel and its vaults, but the geology underpinning them, and when we do we find rumours and legends of caverns and tunnels, both natural and artificial, forming a subterranean labyrinth that spreads for miles in all directions. A few years ago the lintel above one of the doors cracked due to subsidence and the Rosslyn Chapel Trust tried to recover the cost of the repairs from the local coal mine. The Scottish Coal Board denied any liability and produced drawings and maps proving that they had no subterranean shafts below the land on which the Chapel stands. On the other hand, a Roman Catholic care home in the nearby (and similar sounding) village of Rosewell successfully sued the Coal Board for damage to their property caused by mining subsidence. This does not, of course, mean that there are no tunnels under the Chapel for there is ample anecdotal evidence of several such tunnels running from Rosslyn Castle to the Chapel, and also to Hawthornden Castle, which is owned by the Heinz food corporation, and used as an artistic retreat.

It is also interesting to note that the Esk Valley, which is located far below the east end of the Chapel, is often the location of earth lights and other electromagnetic anomalies associated with tectonic movements and piezo electricity, significantly the valley and the nearby Roslin wood are also associated with various occult ceremonies and rites. It has been alleged that in the late 19th century, a piper was put into the cavern system below Rosslyn castle to make his way to Hawthornden Castle playing his pipes as he did so. The piper was never seen again. While this story might be apocryphal there is a similar and slightly better corroborated tale of a piper who was put into the tunnels running out from below Edinburgh Castle and reputedly stretching to Holyrood House. Evidently the idea was to follow the piper's progress from above ground by tracking the sound of the pipes. However, the piping stopped abruptly and when a search party was sent to look for the unfortunate piper he had completely vanished and was never seen again. In fact the idea that castles have escape tunnels is true for practically all major ancient military installations. Stirling Castle, which dates back to the end of the first millennium, is another example of this and it would seem strange if there were not. The garrison might be well defended and provisioned, but it would, sooner or later, be deemed necessary that contact be made with allies outside the castle walls and the only sensible and secure method would be by underground escape routes.

It is further claimed that Crichton Castle is also joined by a network of tunnels and caverns to both Rosslyn Castle and Hawthornden Castle. Stranger still, it was also claimed by an hotelier and Rosslyn researcher, the late Steven Prior, that immediately before the suppression of the Templars in 1307 some of the valuables held in the Preceptories was hastily removed and transported by ship, and landed near the town of Gullane, which is close to Edinburgh on the east coast of Scotland. Mr Prior, who also purported to have been the head of parapsychology for MI5, claimed to have been in possession of papers indicating that the Vatican wanted to obtain the Templar booty. The hotel in Gullane owned by Mr Prior was, perhaps appropriately, called the *Templar Lodge Hotel* and it was also reputedly the site of a former Templar priory. Mr Prior claimed that part of the Templar treasure was transported via a combined system of caverns and tunnels directly to Rosslyn Chapel.

To be fair, this tunnel system must be remarkably extensive and is part of another tunnel network under the Lothians village of Cousland. It is also suggested that the tunnel system encompasses Yester Castle, close to the town of Gifford, and is ancestral home of the Clan Hay. In an example of synchronicity Yester Castle is, in addition, the location of the notorious 'Goblin Hall', or ('Goblin Ha'). This is accessed by a stone lined tunnel underneath the castle and is said to have been constructed by the so-called wizard of Yester, Sir Hugo de Gifford. The Goblin Hall is reputedly partially natural, having been constructed from an existing cavern and was allegedly used by Sir Hugo, regarded a demonologist of some note, to conduct arcane ceremonies and rituals. The castle, which became the seat of Clan Hay in the 14th century, is now a ruin, but the hall still remains. This is sealed off by a heavy, locked iron gate, which was installed for reasons of safety in the past fifty years. Its last recorded use was when it served as the home of the falconer to the Marquis of Tweedale as late as 1737, after which time, like the castle, it was abandoned to its fate.

The mention of magical rituals and the presence of 'demons' in the Goblin Hall, and the fact that it appears to be tied into a much larger cavern system, leads one to speculate on the nature of these so-called 'demons'. Taking a leap of faith one might justifiably consider the possibility that these entities may have been either dwellers from beneath the Earth's surface, or, extraterrestrials. One has only to look at traditional representations of demons and ETs to see the many points of similarity, and given the abject superstition of people during this dark era they would automatically assume anything out of their ken had, of necessity, to be supernatural and therefore demonic. Whatever their nature, if Sir Hugo de Gifford was in contact with them, he must have had both nerves of steel and a damned good reason.

Chapter 19
Through the Doorway

This was first time I had worked with this particular medium, but as we shall see his talent is truly remarkable. I first encountered Patrick McNamara, a businessman and antiques dealer who has his own psychic development circle, during an 'off the cuff' series of experiments using photographs of 'orbs' taken during various investigations at reputedly haunted locations. I deliberately gave very little background information concerning the photographs, and in one memorable example none at all, but the impressions that Patrick discerned from the pictures was genuinely remarkable and in the instance of the picture with no information at all, the results were little short of amazing.

The picture, supplied with absolutely no provenance whatsoever, was taken in the confines of the world famous, 'Mary Kings Close' in Edinburgh and showed the entry passageway, which in this instance was swarming with 'spirit orbs'. Patrick's impressions of this image were absolutely accurate and his description of the conditions that must have been prevalent when the area was occupied was uncanny. It was the result of this brief experiment that convinced me to send him a further image taken within the Chapel. I should add that although the impressions he received are abundant, due to their obvious broad based relevance I have included them in full.

The Picture of the Altar

As mentioned previously, the image I sent Patrick for examination was taken within Rosslyn Chapel in October 2005 and shows the so-called Astral Doorway. It is in fact a picture of the small St Matthew Altar with the adjacent, rectangular metal plate set in the floor in front of the altar, which marks the burial vault of a member of the Sinclair family. The term, Astral Doorway, may be slightly off-putting at first because it carries a certain amount of baggage with it, but it is also reasonable to refer to it as a dimensional gateway or portal. I must make it abundantly clear that at this point Patrick had never been to Scotland, never mind Rosslyn Chapel, so his first impressions were genuinely remarkable. What follows is extracted verbatim (and with permission) from a series of emails written by Patrick in Jan 2006 giving his initial impressions gleaned from the photograph. Bear in mind that due to the nature of the task and its location much of the imagery is powerful and replete with religious symbolism.

First Impressions

'When I first opened this picture, it got very cold around the computer with a strong draught, and my pulse is racing fast.

The first thing I got was a drinking goblet, the sort of thing you would use in a mass. I know it's a church, but that was what hit me the minute I looked at it.

I can see that there is one Knight Templar, wearing the templar cross. I feel this is nearby the grave. There is a white light coming from the grave, a spiritual light.

I get the name "Joseph of Aramathea" and it also feels like a holy order of monks. Someone has shouted out catholic. There is a biblical figure that looks almost Arthurian.

At the headstone I can see a man with a moustache and beard and long collar length hair. I feel he has a biblical presence, or certainly professed to be spiritual. He looks like a well groomed man, a 1930's description of a medieval nobleman. His hair curls under his jaw like in the medieval period.

I get the name Rose Egromont, or perhaps Egrement, (It sounds like this)

Now I get a blonde haired woman holding her throat saying that she was strangled. She says she came from York. The strange thing with this grave is that it feels like a dimensional doorway as I see lots of spirits walking through it, and out of it. I would say it's a spiritual vortex. There really is great energy coming from this tomb.

There is talk about the Temple. The Temple wall. There is an old style document with figures on it. These are like measurements (code) written in a script style writing like on velum.

I see a wall with a crack in it and what looks like a mummified hand. It could be a relic.

I can see a large binding cloth or shroud (Like the Turin shroud.)

Somebody is here talking about people being slaughtered.

I can see flames.

I am getting some kind of tomb within a tomb, a secret. I am also seeing a ring; this ring was a ring of office and would have been very important. I have just been presented with a rose. The rose seems to be changing colour from red to white.

There is a royal connection, not a king or queen, but status of Duke or Earl...Could be a prince. I get the impression of some young people who were going to be powerful but they were killed before their time. Young aristocracy fighting between themselves.

I am being told that they buried the wrong person, it is not who it's supposed to be. I feel there is a secret, something is hidden.

While the above seems to be of an older period, I get a man in 20th century clothes. The period of dress would be around 1930's. I Believe his first name was Harry, and I think the surname begins with P. He had something to do with this site when he was alive. In his hand there is a pen, so he may have written about this place and been a writer.

On a separate note I see big red velvet curtains. A guide here is talking about a chandelier or light fitting being changed. Certainly something to do with lighting.

Something happens on an anniversary.

Within this location I see that a lady in white visits and two young brothers who seem to haunt the place. I see masses of flowers with this.

A set of cross keys is being presented.

I see a skull on it's own without a skeleton.

Somebody is blowing a horn...

This initial response from Patrick to the image of the small altar and vault is remarkable and many of the images have deep religious and spiritual significance and are worth examining in some detail. The first impression he obtained was of a strong, cold draught of air around the computer when he downloaded the image. This is exactly what was felt by those who stood on the vault during the first evaluation and also, of course, during the second visit after initiating the specific musical tones on the laptop computer. His impressions, even although they were conveyed via a computer link, are absolutely valid, the method of producing the image is not relevant but the image is.

The mention of a Templar Knight is also excellent; there are at least ten members of the Sinclair family (although to be fair not all were Templars) said to be buried in the main Chapel vaults in full armour. It is certain that there was a strong Templar connection with the Sinclair family, especially when the Chapel was constructed. The impression of monks is also absolutely correct, the Templar order was an organisation both mentored and sponsored by the Catholic Church; in addition they were, in effect warrior monks. To be strictly accurate, this description may have been the case when they were originally created, but prior to their dissolution the order had become largely answerable to no one but itself and its grandmaster, and was effectively above the law. The figure at the headstone is something of a puzzle although to be expected, it carries strong resonances with what the mediums discerned during the original visit in 1998, a guardian of some sort.

The use of the expression, 'Rose Egromont,' is more enigmatic and might refer to a number of things including the Ros in Rosslyn, however the word, Rose, may indicate secrecy because the rose was a traditional symbol often use to imply secrecy, it also might mean the 'Rose Line', the theoretical line running from the beautiful Chartres Cathedral in Paris to Rosslyn Chapel outside Edinburgh. The word, 'Egromont,' sounds vaguely French, but other than a possible link to Chartres there is nothing definite here.

The mention of a blond haired woman is too ephemeral, but the observation about the dimensional doorway and spiritual vortex is astounding and agrees precisely with what the mediums originally discerned in 1998. The only slight difference is in the vocabulary used to describe it, Patrick uses the terms 'dimensional doorway' and 'vortex', where the first set of psychics call it an 'Astral Doorway'. In effect there is no difference at all; the function it serves is identical. Patrick talks about the temple wall and a wall with crack in it: could this be a reference to the claims that the west wall of Rosslyn although claimed to be the abandoned attempt to build a transept, was in truth an attempt by William Sinclair to recreate the ruined west wall of Solomon's temple in Jerusalem?

This concept is thoroughly explored and elaborated upon in the excellent work on the origins of Freemasonry, *The Hiram Key* by Lomas and Knight. The mention of a mummified hand as a relic is not surprising since the practise of venerating assorted dubious relics was common practise during the Middle Ages, although there is no specific reference to Rosslyn having a relic. The rather grisly practise of venerating relics, and occasionally the mummified body of a saint, still happens today, but the practise is less common than it was.

The reference to slaughter and flames may well be direct reference to the siege of nearby Rosslyn Castle by the soldiers under General Monk during the Civil War, when the Chapel was used as a stable for their horses. It could also refer to the sacking of the Chapel by Protestant mobs during The Reformation in Scotland. The mention of a 'tomb within a tomb' may be highly significant, especially with its mention of a secret. Oddly enough this same image was given by a transfiguration medium during a public demonstration a few weeks later in January 2006, when I asked a question of him while he was in trance. The question was deliberately general and non-specific and produced a series of answers all relating to aspects of the Rosslyn project, particularly the secret. Once again a rose is mentioned, perhaps yet another veiled reference to secrecy and the mention of minor royalty and princes; this has to be the thread of nobility in the Sinclair family in general, not just Sir William Sinclair, who as we have seen, was the third and last Prince of Orkney and the title of Prince was hereditary and would have passed down within his family.

The mention of the 1930s is odd, but when Patrick refers to a man with the first name of Harry and a second name beginning with the letter 'P,' the logical assumption here is that he talks about the legendary (or perhaps notorious) ghost hunter of the period Harry Price. Harry Price made his reputation by investigating claims of the repeated and systematic haunting of the now destroyed Borley Rectory, at the time called 'The most haunted house in England'. While it is not known if Price actually visited the Chapel, neither is it impossible, certainly the time and initials fit. The reference to a pen and writing also are relevant to this hypothesis as Price wrote up and published many of his cases, especially his long-term investigations at Borley. The mention of red drapes refers to the coverings in the Chapel altars and astonishingly the observation about the lighting is absolutely correct. On one of our visits immediately prior to the November investigation, my wife and I were told that there was electrical work being undertaken on the lighting in the Chapel.

When Patrick talks of cross keys being presented, this might refer to an exchange of information or the means of revealing a secret. It might also refer to one of the bas-relief carvings on the walls of the crypt that clearly depict a saint bearing a large set of crossed keys; the skull without a skeleton however is another matter entirely, another reference to a hidden relic or possibly something else. This just might refer to the fascinating theory that the mummified head of Jesus Christ is cached inside the Apprentice Pillar, that enigmatic and beautiful stone column located at one side of the Lady Chapel. On the other hand is it possible that this refers to one of the heresies with which the Templars were charged; i.e. that they worshipped a mysterious head called the 'Baphomet'?

This artefact has frequently been speculated upon and one interpretation appears to be part of the trappings of cults who worshipped the human head as the seat of the soul. Once again the transfiguration medium also mentioned the presence of a skull and some bones wrapped in a cloth. The association with the Knights Templar and their alleged connection with Rosslyn through the Sinclairs is also a possibility, but as with many of the legends surrounding this mystical organisation, it is difficult to prove. There are abundant references to this from a variety of sources, but in all cases the evidence is either speculative or hearsay. What evidence there is appears to have been gleaned under torture from some of the Templars after their dissolution in 1307, and the value of this is, therefore, open to debate.

Chapter 20
The Second Communication

What follows is once again from Patrick and his observations are particularly revealing.

I have been through the doorway. It is dimensional and it links different times or different dimensions of time together. You know how when I look at a photograph, I get a connection almost like Psychometry, well in this case I am getting lots of different moving pictures and they don't just relate to the picture I was looking at last night. This man in the headstone seems to be a link, or guardian, and most of these impressions come through or from him, he is that powerful. This is the man I mentions who has the beard and moustache and looks medieval. He has piercing green coloured eyes. (Authors note: the word 'psychometry' used above describes a divinatory technique used by a psychic to obtain impressions of various kinds after handling an artefact belonging to another person whether dead or alive)

I got a vortex, or dimensional doorway, whereby you could go back in time, or people could send thoughts forward from what we call the past. Within this vortex it is like a circle of people, who were directing thoughts and forces through this doorway. I got "Grand Master" and there is a force of occult power, which can be called on by certain people. It is almost as though there was a whole network of people down through the centuries who have one constructive idea or program. If you are called to use this energy, you can connect with all the different centuries. This is a collective energy or force, which can be used by these individuals. I can see thought forms where it is almost like a magical force. This is ritual power. It is very difficult to explain.

Within the doorway there are really powerful emotions present, and when I connected with this thought energy in the different time periods, there was an immense amount of passion and emotion that came out from it, that could be almost overwhelming. I was picking up on the thoughts and emotions from these individuals. They also showed me what looked like a stained glass window that kept being smashed and replaced each time with a different picture on it. But, it seems as though there is an energy source directed at a particular group of sensitives, or people involved in the occult sciences, to a very high standard of involvement. I had a feeling of almost magical powers with these people. I can't explain it as I don't know much about this occult practice, or the magic involved, but I know very well that it does work. I keep seeing a cross, but it's an unusual cross. And a rose once again as last night. I am getting a light that looks almost like a pink laser. They are telling me that if you use certain lights this will help to open the vortex so that you can see, feel and hear more.

I have done experiment with lights in my physical circle, but this is different. I am getting sounds coming to my ear as I mention this, as though you could enhance whatever you are working on, as I have no idea, by using different lights and sounds at different frequencies. I wish I could help more but the link is good, but not the same as the physical presence.

I am getting the name again, Joseph, Joseph. I have a strange feeling in my stomach.

One other thing, I am seeing an image of what looks like dead knights with the Templars cross. As I see them, it is as though they are getting up and rising from the dead, like they were sleeping. They are described as guardians. I get a feeling of hatred for religion and especially the Catholics. Joseph is saying "death to the pope", it is said like a curse. A man is saying that there is a hidden vault. And he is showing me treasure within this vault.... I get a strong feeling with this that may not be gold and jewels, but a spiritual treasure. This man is incredibly powerful. As I link my body is shaking. Once again as with last night, I see this ring. These knights are not from England, but a foreign country. These men were hunted down. Psychically I would say this link is very, very, strong.

Lastly, I am being shown a tree, not sure what type it is, but it is not English and has odd leaves on it.

P.S. I have "sound resonance" called out.

Once again, Patrick's perceptions are truly remarkable, especially his reference to a Grand Master and 'occult power' that, over the years, may be used and directed by a select few. He refers to 'thought forms' being like a magical force, this may be a reference to a 'sigil', which is the written essence of a spell or word of power reduced down to its very purest and potent form, it is at the core of chaos magic. It is rather like producing a stock or gravy during cooking by boiling off all the unnecessary fluid leaving behind the most concentrated parts of the components in the recipe. When he talks about ritual power, this is exactly what is involved in creating the necessary conditions to activate to latent energy in the Chapel.

The mention of powerful emotions is also highly relevant to what he is looking at, as is the implication that they are from different time periods. The introduction of windows being smashed and replaced with a different picture appears to corroborate what was said by the medium about the windows in the Chapel changing, almost from day to day during the first evaluation in 1998. Remember that the images seen are not necessarily identical and may require some interpretation. He returns to the impression of magic and energy being used by a group of people, he describes them as using 'occult sciences', which is an apt description for magic is science by any other name. Patrick talks about an unusual cross, is this the Ankh, the symbol of life?

Once again the rose symbol appears and in addition a pink light exhibiting properties similar to a laser. His guides tell him that using light at different (red?) frequencies may be helpful in opening the doorway. Anyone who has ever attended a séance will know that the only colours of light allowed in a séance room are red, or in some cases blue. These are images being presented to the medium and it is odd, or perhaps revealing, that they should all be within the red spectrum of light. This might be a hint that if only red lights (in the main) are used while mediums are working with 'spirit', then this must also refer to the nature of the material universe which consists, down to its last subatomic particle, entirely of frequency and resonance. If spirit finds it difficult to operate in visible (white) light, then obviously some frequencies of light are either inimical or inhibiting for it. While I have already mentioned that for all the claimed spirit activity detected within the Chapel, there have never been any images of orbs captured in any of the hundreds of photographs and video tapes taken during the investigations. This was the case until I received one image that was shot in March 2006 by a visitor to the Chapel who got in touch and sent me the images they had taken. It clearly shows a pink orb and was taken close to the Lady Chapel. This unusual picture also seems to bear out Patrick's observations concerning a pink light.

At the close of the second email Patrick begins to mention hearing sounds and receiving images of dead knights with the unique Templar *croix pattée*, he interprets them as sleeping guardians. He also hears the Catholic Church being railed against and castigated; he hears a Joseph (is this the aforementioned Joseph of Aramathea?) saying, *'Death to the Pope'*, but this is unlikely given the timeline. However, while all of this might refer to the abolition of the Templar order, it might also refer to the Scottish Reformation of the churches and the ascendancy of the Protestant version of Christianity. Once again there is reference to a hidden vault and treasure but implying that it is a spiritual not physical treasure.

Again Patrick sees a ring, is it the fisherman's ring of the Pope? Or could it be the cipher of another mystical and esoteric society, perhaps the Rex Deus families, a shadowy but influential group who are reputedly descended from the priests who served in Solomon's Temple in ancient Israel? He detects knights but from a foreign country, but they are being hunted and sought after, are they the French Knights that comprised those who fled France immediately after the Templar suppression of 13th October 1307? Finally he comes to what is perhaps one of the two main keys in solving the puzzle; it is what was revealed to us during the sonic valuation at Rosslyn Chapel in November 2005. He hears 'sound resonance' called out; this is exactly what I had deduced regarding the information encoded into the decorative cubes located in the ceiling of the Lady Chapel.

One of Patrick's later observations concerns the location of a device, a physical object, that he believes will assist in creating the correct conditions to open the doorway, he thinks this object is what is hidden in the 'box within a box'. He also says quite clearly that this object will help reproduce the sounds and frequencies necessary to unlock the door. Once the door is open, it will release a set of energies that will enable the use of abilities such as speaking in tongues, prophecy, levitation and as if this was not enough, dimensional time travel; the original purpose of the doorway. Another observation was perhaps particularly closer to the mark, I had repeatedly asked Patrick what, if anything, was hidden through the doorway and he replied, '*Knowledge*'.

This explanation is, if one thinks about it, remarkably close to the nature of The Baphomet, at least in two of its guises, viz. '*The father of universal peace among men*', and Abu-fihamat, i.e. '*father of understanding*'. Is the concealed item therefore a state of mind or a spiritual condition rather than a thing? In fact, it sounds in many ways like a definition of what madam Helen Blavatski, founder of the Theosophical movement, referred to as the 'Akashic Records'. In other words an infinite library comprising all the knowledge, thoughts and experience acquired by the human race since time began; some even speculate that it also contains knowledge of the future; all that has been, is, and will be, just waiting to be accessed and used for good or ill. This is also sometimes referred to as the collective unconscious or universal mind. In another sense it seems to define what Dr. Rupert Sheldrake called 'morphogenetic fields', or an ever evolving field of information that appears to directly affect what we do and think, and more importantly is affected in turn by what we as a species learn.

Once again we are confronted by a choice; either a variant of the duality of Rosslyn Chapel, viz. the secret of Rosslyn is knowledge and not necessarily spiritual knowledge, or, it is the nature of the doorway itself, a transit point for spirit, or a 'way station' for the use of entities making a longer journey? Other mediums tell us that the doorway is potentially dangerous and a possible entry point for beings that may be inimical to humanity. They also tell us that the doorway is very much a two way opening, things both physical and non physical can pass through freely from either direction and herein lies its greatest hazard. The mediums also tell us that there is a guardian permanently on duty monitoring what happens at the portal, we cannot see or hear him, but nevertheless he is there.

In the weeks following the introduction of Patrick McNamara to the mysteries of the Chapel he requested a copy of the frequencies we had used during our November visit. I had originally produced a CD featuring all the frequencies relevant to the Chapel plus those constituting the Solfeggio frequencies. Following that, Patrick listened to them and selected those that had the most profound affect upon him. I then re-recorded a CD of three specific tones each of 15 minutes duration and following a number of tests he performed both on himself and a psychic colleague. The following results emerged. The final selection of tones comprised the original Devils Chord i.e. F# = 370 Hz C = 523Hz A = 880Hz, an alternate tone consisting of two frequencies, i.e. F#, 370 Hz and C, 523 Hz and finally the single central note from the Solfeggio frequencies, i.e. 528 Hz. What follows is an account from Patrick of the effects of the tones:

Test 1 *(1) Devils chord (abb)– 370, 523. Seemed to increase clairvoyant ability and seems to aid physical mediumship. When this tone is played after 10 minutes two mediums were aware of a presence, in this case it was a templar. There was also a presence of nature spirits which I was aware of and moved at very fast speeds. They seemed to be able to use tone one to increase their presence.*

(2) Sol frequencies – *396, 417, 528, 693, 741, 852. Aided trance ability, feelings of withdrawal and pin and needles in the hands. Certainly aids deep relaxation. Seems to cause muscle contractions in the arms and legs of both mediums. Did start to produce energy from ears and nose. There was definite increase in psychic activity, including cold drafts. Mild nausea and discomfort with this near the end. In general there is a definite expansion of psychic ability with all of the tones, but each does have a different affect. There was some knocking and tapping.*

Test 2 *(1) Devils Chord (org) - Did not notice anything of significance.*

(2) Gematria Equivalent - 373, 515, 888 Hz - More heightened senses. Felt ectoplasm coming out of my nose. I believe I heard voices of women chatting in the distance. Seems to be inductive to trance as I fell into a semi trance state. Saw visions of people sitting down around tables, like a large gathering to eat and drink together.
(3) Trans/Miracles – 528hz I would definitely add, that the trance feeling was possibly heightened with this tone, as I jumped back into my body when the tone stopped.

Why should these frequencies have such a strange affect on human beings in general and mediums in particular? What is the relationship between specific frequencies and the ability to experience transcended states? The answer apparently lies in the neurological processes of the human brain and what happens to them under suitable stimulation. This peculiar relationship between sound and perception has been successfully exploited commercially by, for example, the Munro Institute in the USA where it was developed into a technique called '*Hemi-synch*', which is a contraction of '*hemispherical synchronisation*'. This technology, which attempts to synchronise the two hemispheres of the brain, hence 'hemi-synch', appears to be a further development of accepted motivational techniques that have been available for some time as audiotapes employing a measure of suggestion and hypnosis to induce positive responses in the user/ This can be anything from losing weight to stopping smoking, or, indeed, inducing out of body experiences.

In the case of Hemi-synch, two sounds of very slightly different frequencies are generated and individually applied to the left and right ear of the user, normally by headphones. For the effect to be successful the tones have to be less that 1500Hz in frequency and the difference between them has to be less than 30Hz otherwise the brain can hear it, thus rendering the effect useless. However, if for example one frequency is 500Hz and the other is 510 Hz, then the heterodyne frequency is 10Hz, which is part of the Alpha wave frequencies of 7–13hz. When the correct frequencies are applied separately to each ear, the brain acts as an organic heterodyne device and creates a third tone, which is called a binaural beat. These frequencies are generated naturally while the brain is in a state of wakeful relaxation. The effect was discovered, or perhaps that should be re-discovered, in 1839 by Heinrich Dove, but it appears that our ancient ancestors originally discovered it by accident and used it instinctively after refining it by observation, trial and error.

In scientific terms, the brain is actually made to track the frequencies it hears because they operate at the same frequency as the brain itself when it enters different states, the process is called 'entrainment' through a naturally occurring frequency following response. The specific frequencies range from 13–40 Hz (Beta Waves) for an attentive state, through 13–40 Hz (Alpha Waves) for wakeful relaxation and on to 4–7 Hz (Theta Waves) for dreams and deep meditation, then, finally to less than 4Hz (Delta Waves) for deep sleep. All of the last three sets of frequencies produce feelings of relaxation and tranquillity but particularly the Alpha and Delta states; it is here that both 'Out of Body' experiences and 'psychic' events are reported.

It is interesting to note that for children under the age of five the expanded consciousness alpha brain state is quite normal while awake in their daily life and this may well be a contributing factor to the observation that young children frequently observe beings and entities not normally visible to adults. The fact that adults cannot see them does not of course mean that they are not there, merely that they are effectively filtered out. It may also explain the often-recorded phenomenon of 'invisible friends' who frequently become their playmates. Regrettably, in adolescence the human brain evolves naturally into the 'normal' adult beta state, which can only be pushed aside with assistance; the only time this happens involuntarily is while sleeping.

Lastly, another commercial adjunct to induced relaxation is the use of specially designed goggles and visors incorporating lights, usually light emitting diodes, flickering at specific frequencies to either induce altered states on their own or enhance altered states of consciousness, and visionary episodes previously indices by the use of sound alone. It may be highly relevant that Patrick specifically mentions the use of sound *and also light* to open the doorway. Why should this be relevant to Rosslyn Chapel? If we recall the peculiar sonic effect that occurred in October 2005 when The Devil's Chord was reproduced in the Chapel while Nathan Surea 'toned' in the crypt, the two tones produced another two quite separate notes, astonishingly; and purely as a result of its proportion and design including the scalloped contours of the of the Sinclairs enGrailed cross, the Chapel was acting as a heterodyne device and automatically producing the third tone, this is little short of astounding! This has to be directly attributable to the use of the Golden Ratio of 1.681 in the construction of the Chapel and the probable reason that The Devil's Chord was proscribed in Europe.

Whatever the effect, what follows is another verbatim account of a trance session undertaken using the frequencies, this time it involved Patrick and an associate of his, another medium named Mr Karl Fallon, Karl wrote Patrick's words down as he spoke them and they are reprinted here with their full permission. In the vision that follows, among other things Patrick sees an etheric entity, a knight, indicating three musical tones, is this a reference to the bizarre heterodyne effect apparently inherent in the Chapel?

Patrick describes the spirit

I have a Templar Knight who has just appeared in front of me. He is standing tall with his hands resting on his sword. He is telling me to write this down. (Karl quickly take up a pen and some paper).

Rosslyn: Between Two Worlds

Patrick speaks: *The notes you have found were used by the Templars to open people's minds. There are other notes yet to be discovered. There is also a connection between the tones and what you term occult magic. The tones were used to open doorways, not only spiritual doorways, but doorways to the minds. There is a small box hidden somewhere in the Chapel, (we were not told where yet) and once this box is found there are keys that can be turned which will give a link to how the notes should be placed together and used for various magical purposes. These purposes would be known to you as placing of curses, casting of spells, and what you term calling up lower spirits.*

The tones are also used for opening up dimensional doorways so that certain rays can be connected to individuals for prophecy, healing, speaking in tongues, wisdom, courage, and the power of fury, allowing terrible spirits of great force who would add courage or great viciousness to an individual. This gives you power of arms that you would have never learnt before and making you become a fighting machine of great power and horror. All these things are possible. To use these powers you need to know the combinations and have strength of mind to control them. The small box mentioned already, is hidden, but I am not telling where it is yet. There is also a hidden chamber, which contains other secrets.

Patrick describes an object being shown: *I am being shown what look like large crystals. From these crystals different coloured lights are emanating. I am getting an intense feeling from this Templar guide. I am now being shown a knights coif on his head. He puts his hands to ears to cover them and warns that you should be wary of these tones. They are very powerful. He is showing three fingers on his hand, and tapping them on his hand while moving his fingers in a rhythmic motion. This is meant to describe three different tones, which can be used to create a harmonic sound. I can see a map of the countryside laid out in front of the knight with a blue print of the building in the middle of it. From the middle of the map, there is a star shape emanating out and the Chapel is the focal centre of it. It seems as though that something has been buried, or built, where the tips of the stars end. I feel this star shape is like a pentagram. The feeling I get while linking with this person is quite painful; my neck is tense and stiff with my eyes watering. My stomach has a giddy feeling.*

Karl asks: *Do you get a name with this knight.*

Patrick asks for a name: *I am getting the name Spencer.*

At this point the trance session concluded.

What Patrick sensed is entirely in keeping with his other attempts to analyse what is present in the Chapel. It is however very difficult to quantify. In cases like this one must rely entirely on the veracity of what the medium says, because there is little or no way to prove what he is sensing. The name of the knight, Spencer, although it could not be traced, may or may not be relevant because there has been so much history involving the building, and the continued Templar imagery is also difficult to prove because there is so much divergence of opinion concerning the Templar presence at Rosslyn.

This is, of course, not to say that it is impossible, but it is more likely that the presence of an armoured Templar Knight complete with a sword may be symbolic and an indication of the political and religious sympathies of the Sinclair family. The reference to the tones and frequencies is encouraging and may indicate that the use of specific tones within the Chapel is significant. It may be relevant that he received the impression that the tones should be used with great care. His description of crystals and lights and the mention of the word, 'occult', is rather more worrying, but there have been many suggestions that the Knights Templar did in fact adopt several practises that are normally associated with magic, and its associated ceremonies.

In April 2006 we visited the Chapel again, this time as normal, paying visitors and took with us another medium, a Mr Adrian Turpin. Mr Turpin's comments tended to be slightly more general and at first concentrated on the spirit presences tied to the Chapel, although he did eventually locate the presence of the 'doorway' adjacent to the St Matthew Altar in the north east corner of the Lady Chapel. In addition to this he also stated that there were five vortices in total within the body of the building, three in the Lady Chapel, one in the quire, (or main section) of the Chapel, and another in the crypt.

It is interesting to note that he became decidedly uneasy while in the location of the 'main' vortex and moved away from this area as it was making him feel ill, an effect that was noted and shared by a friend of his who was present. A trip down into the crypt did not produce any additional information other than the location of the crypt also induced sensations of nausea, which was attributed to the presence of ley lines. From my perspective it was gratifying that another medium should pick up on the significance of the small, otherwise unremarkable area in the north east of the building. It is also interesting to note that when they were in the crypt, Adrian located the additional area of potential energy in an alcove on the north wall.

Chapter 21
The Red Light

As you will recall in the previous chapter, the medium Patrick McNamara mentioned the presence of what he described as a 'pink laser'. While that was astonishing and thought provoking enough, I had no idea what was to follow a few months later after the publication of this book. Out of the blue and into my inbox, came an email from Marcel Leroux who hales from Connecticut in the USA, and what he had to say really set me back on my heels. Marcel had bought a copy of the book and, after reading it, out of sheer curiosity he decided to dowse a plan of the Chapel.

Here he located two hidden objects that, in his opinion, are additional secrets; in this case they are physical artefacts. Marcel believes they resemble calculating devices of some kind. From the way he described them and from the drawings he sent me (see plates) they could almost resemble a cross between a slide-rule and calculator. They are tubes comprising two separate sections, one designed to fit snugly inside the other, but still able to move freely up and down. The inner and outer are engraved with figures and symbols of some kind, but the truly fascinating thing is that, again according to Marcel, they are intended to be read using coherent light, i.e. laser light.

I am aware that the first lasers designed for commercial use were ruby lasers of the kind found in the laser pens used to highlight parts of a PowerPoint or slide presentation. The first success with a laser was in 1960 at the Hughes Research Laboratory in California, by shining a high-power light on a ruby rod with silver-coated surfaces. In fact it was the inestimable Albert Einstein who first came up with the idea at the beginning of the 20th century, when in 1917 he introduced the concept of the stimulated emission of photons interacting with excited molecules or atoms and causing the emission of a second photon of the same frequency, polarization and direction.

This is all well and good, but what would that have to do with ancient technology allegedly hidden in the fabric of Rosslyn Chapel that needed coherent light to be read; where would that come from? As it happens the answer presented itself in a truly spectacular example of synchronicity, a phenomenon which I am convinced is much more than sheer happenstance, and which I have experienced many times in the course of my research.

For many months I had thought long and hard about Marcel's claims, especially about the aspect of coherent light, it seemed to be a real stumbling block, when, as if by magic, the answer presented itself to me in a discovery made by a researcher of anomalies, Alan Butler, and Rosslyn expert John Ritchie (who is the media officer of the *Militi Templi Scotia* i.e the modern Scottish Knights Templar). A long forgotten part of the Rosslyn saga was rediscovered immediately above the Rose Window at the east end of the Chapel; this was a long forgotten 'light box'.

This is a red crystal of some kind set in a reflective (probably mica) lined pentagonal aperture that was designed to allow a narrow beam of red light into the building, particularly at sunrise of specific days of the year. It now seems that this lightbox last functioned as intended in the year 1844 when the present Rose Window was remodelled. According to local lore, some of the older residents of Roslin village talk about a mysterious red light that used to appear on the 21st of September which is St Matthew's Day. We should never forget that despite its better known title of Rosslyn Chapel, it is also, and more correctly, referred to as The Collegiate Church of St Matthew.

In any event Mr Ritchie actually tested the lightbox to see if it still functioned. He did this by purchasing a very powerful torch and climbing up on the scaffolding that was there as part of an ongoing restoration project. When he shone the powerful beam through the aperture, instead of a weak, insipid spot of white light there was a bright, strong orb of crimson light projected into the Chapel. After five hundred years it functioned exactly as its designer intended. In fact, the lightbox would have functioned as intended twice a year, once on the 21st of March (the first day of spring) and also on the 21st of September, which in addition to being St Matthew's Day is also the Autumn Equinox. There may even be a connection to the All Seeing Eye of Freemasonry.

It is thought that until the window was remodelled, the light would have shone on a specific spot on the floor, although just what was supposed to be illuminated is uncertain. Perhaps it indicated that something very special indeed was under that spot, but we just don't know and the trustees are in no hurry to find out. Is it possible that the devices that Marcel Leroux is sure are hidden in the Chapel are the very devices intended to be illuminated by this beam of red light? Of course it does not qualify as a laser, but the similarities are astounding. Sadly it is doubtful if this theory will ever be put to the test. This is for no other reason than, if actually there, Marcel's remarkable artefacts would have to be excavated from the fabric of the building, and that is unlikely to happen anytime soon.

Chapter 22
The Apostle James sends a Warning

Powerful stuff indeed, but is it valid? As we have seen, there is, once again repeated mention of specific musical notation and as we have already learned, music, or, more correctly, frequency, comprises the key that will eventually unlock whatever arcane knowledge is concealed there. However, the story does not stop here and what follows was received quite unexpectedly and completely unsolicited via an email from the USA which arrived in April 2006. It came from the Reverend James Collier, a lay preacher who prefers to be known as the Apostle James, and at his specific request I shall respect this and use the term of address. Some of the implications of this communication are quite alarming. Once again, as with the other interested parties, the Apostle James gave his permission for the slightly edited correspondence to be reprinted here.

What is presented is just one of many synchronicities that have occurred since I first began researching the enigmas present within Rosslyn Chapel. It is also only one of several cautionary messages I received in relation to what we had attempted in the Chapel with the frequencies, and it is another example of what can only be described as 'spiritual interaction' that had come my way since 2004. I should make clear that the Apostle James uses an evangelical, charismatic style of ministry; prior knowledge of this fact may make his interpretation more accessible to the reader, however this does not automatically preclude him from possessing instinctive psychic talents and, as it transpired, they are very well honed indeed.

The Apostle James writes: *I pray all is well with you and bid you Shalom! (Peace) I am a Holy man who walks in the office of Apostle. Often, the Lord gives me dreams. They always pertain to the things to come, as we near times of Great Tribulation. Recently, however, He gave me a dream of something that has already happened. Two months ago on Feb. 20th, I had been praying about the coming anti-Christ. This will be a person that will be possessed with Satan's spirit. I had been asking the Lord in prayer, when we could expect this to happen. He gave me a quite disturbing dream that night and included in it a date, January 25th 2005. In the dream, I was in an early century Chapel somewhere and a great evil was released by playing some evil music. As soon as I awoke, I wrote the dream down.. I prayed over the meaning of it and a few days later the Lord led me to an article that answered almost all of my questions. (The Devils Symphony)*

After reading the article I searched Google for this Rosslyn Chapel that was mentioned in its text. Upon looking at the interior pictures of this Chapel, I knew it was the one that I had just been in while having this dream. I know what has happened there and I am currently trying to confirm the date. Can you give me any information as to what happened in this Chapel on the day of January 25th 2005? Who was there and what they were doing? It would be most helpful [to know this]. I can confirm to you, because of what the Lord showed me in this dream, that this Devil's Chord is real, the notes are real and something evil has been released from this Chapel. Also, I would like to add that I live in the U.S. and had no prior knowledge of this Chapel or your findings there before the Lord gave me this dream. I pray that I hear from you concerning this. There is something taking place in that Chapel that is more evil than anyone could possibly imagine and it needs to be exposed.

As with what I received from Patrick this message was to the point, but in this case also carries with it the clear warning of impending danger, particularly in respect of the experiments carried out in October 2005, although in fairness this is not the only time that specific types of music has been played or performed in the Chapel. Once again my thoughts returned to the *a cappella* performances in the crypt given in the late 1990s, because Adrian had located a spiritual nexus there, and it is also the location of series of ley lines. Unfortunately there is no way now to tell if these singers had intended rather more than a simple desire to reproduce their music and had, instead attempted to influence the latent energies within the crypt.

My enquiries at the Chapel on behalf of the Apostle regarding the date mentioned, the 25th of January 2005, did not reveal any especially significant information other than there had been a celebration of the works of the world famous Scots poet, Robert Burns, held in the Chapel. However, perhaps we should examine the significance of his dream, and what follows is once again reproduced with his permission. I should point out that Rosslyn Chapel, in order to make financial ends meet, is hired out for a variety of functions. For obvious reasons all of them carefully vetted beforehand because various groups have attempted to conduct ceremonies and rituals in the Chapel, and not all of them particularly wholesome. However, this was not the only communication received from him, and what follows is the transcript of a dream experienced by him and is presented here in a slightly edited form; some of the imagery is both alarming and apocalyptic in nature as befits the Apostle's religious paradigm.

The Dream

As the dream begins, I'm inside an old Chapel. I can tell that it is very old. Early century. I get the feeling of 14th or 15th century. As I look around, I notice a lot of very intricate carvings and mouldings that are on the walls and ceiling. I have never seen anything like it. I also notice the high ceiling and that I am actually in a wing of the Chapel. Now I'm looking over this wooden banister into a balcony area. Standing in the balcony area is a Choir. They are all dressed in early century clothing. They are singing in a foreign language. I get the feeling that it's Italian, it's like an Orchestra. Even though I do not see anybody holding any instruments, I can hear instruments being played. Instruments of all types, like you would normally hear in an orchestra.

As they are singing, these two men stand up, one standing just right behind the other. While everyone else is singing, these two start singing in what sounds like an "Om". It's just a short "Om". Like a Chord. Very deep sounding, a deep bass sound. One man's sound is just slightly deeper than the other man's. I find it to be evil sounding. They just keep alternating back and forth, with these two deep "Om's". As this keeps going on, a Lady stands up on the left side of the Choir and she is singing too. I can't believe what I'm seeing now. Her eyes keep changing! They go from normal to a cloudy white colour, just like you see in the movies, when someone is demonically possessed! Now, I notice that every time the two guys start singing their chords, this is when her eyes change. I'm just standing there amazed. This choir's music, along with these two deep chords are making this Lady become possessed! This music is some kind of key to release something very evil! Now, I look to the left of her and hanging on the wall, behind them is this long banner. All it has on it is a date. January 25th 2005, that's all it has on it and I can read it clearly.

Now I am in a cave or basement under the Chapel. The walls and ceiling are rock, but for some reason I feel like I'm under the Chapel. I am standing in the centre of this huge room holding my daughter. It's very cosy here. I look over across the room and my father is sitting on a couch and is just smiling at me. I look up at the ceiling of this underground room and I see that there is a small square opening. I can see into the sky through it. It's dark outside and I can see a star in the sky. I point to it and tell my daughter, "Look that's Jesus. Jesus is coming!" Now I walk over to a small room. My wife is inside this room spreading out blankets on the floor.

I'm looking around the floor and notice that there are sleeping bags and more blankets. I get the feeling that this is a sleeping area. I get the feeling again that I'm in a very cosy and comfortable place and that we are using it for shelter. From this room, I look out of another small square window and this time it is daytime outside. It is cloudy and there is a light snow falling. Someone says to me, "They say that it could get very bad out. It could possibly dump a couple of feet of snow!" I never get a look at the person who said this. The news doesn't bother me, because I still feel safe and cosy down here.

Now I'm walking through the Chapel again and come to a large room that has several pews in it. There are a lot of people sitting in the pews. They are sitting around and have blankets over them pulled up to their chins. I find this odd, because I don't feel the least bit cold. On the front row I see a place to sit down at the end of the pew. I sit down next to a lady. She has a lot of spare blanket, so I pull it over me and hold on to it. I don't know why, but I do. Now, I realize that everyone is listening to music. I do not see anyone singing or anything, but I hear it. I get the feeling that they are watching a play, but once again, I don't see anything. My wife and kids come up behind me and sit down. They are rather noisy. I turn around and give them a look of, "Could you possibly make any more noise?" My wife tells me that the director said that they didn't have to listen and that it would even be better, if they didn't pay any attention to it at all, because it would just probably distract the kids, when their part comes up. Now, for some reason, I know that my wife is in charge of the kids group and that they just come over to sit down, until it's their time to participate in the play, at this point the dream ended.

The Apostle's dream is exciting and remarkable by any standards and the mention of a choir singing in a foreign language appears to refer to the choir we heard during our first visit in 1998. When this is considered in relation to his description of the elaborate carvings coupled to the description of the interior this does seem to accurately describe Rosslyn. Later in the dream he talks about being in a cavern below the Chapel and of hearing low frequency musical notes, again this seems to describe both the presence of the vaults and a possible former Temple of Mithras, and to our sonic experiments in the Chapel. He also mentions what might refer to the present crypt and its former use as accommodation for the workforce.

The sight of people sitting with blankets wrapped around them is an excellent description of the audience attending one of the many musical and theatrical presentations and performances held in the Chapel. The Chapel is an old, draughty stone building so it is cool even in the summer and in winter it is very cold indeed, so the sight of people keeping warm with blankets comes as no surprise. He tells us that the music produced by the choir combined with the two low frequency tones has an adverse affect on a woman who seems to become possessed, but the mention of evil does seem bizarre since there has at no time been any sense of anything untoward or negative. A day later I received the following communication from him and once again I have edited it slightly, but the message and context have not been altered in any way.

The Next Message
I am still going over all of my notes for the Rosslyn dream. Last night I spent some time with one of my Prophetesses. I mentioned Rosslyn to her and right away she started hearing from the Holy Spirit. She mentioned a portal, a gateway for demons to traverse back and forth, she said that a demon was guarding a portal in a corner, that demons like to hide in corners, she mentioned vaults and asked me how many vaults are under this place. She said all of this, just at hearing the name Rosslyn. I haven't talked to her or [told her] anything about this. She is an older widow that lives in seclusion. She lives in an isolated place in Texas. I know her quite well. I knew she was hearing all of this in the spirit.

I am sending her your articles and directed her to my site, so she could read my dream. I am using her and another spirit filled woman to help confirm some of the things that the Lord has shown me. This is how we maintain Biblical correctness. When the Lord reveals something to His chosen, we find two witnesses to confirm it, before giving the message out. These two women I have sought help with I trust very much, because they know nothing about Rosslyn and I know they walk in the Spirit with the Lord. This is going to be very interesting to hear their responses. You will be the first one to know, as soon as we are done. I feel very comfortable telling you anything that is revealed to us. I will be working on this as quickly as time allows.

What The Apostle says regarding his female colleague who, in any other set of circumstances would be described as a psychic, is genuinely instructive and probably reflects her fundamentalist Christian religious mindset. She sees the portal, but instead of a knight she sees a demon guardian and she also sees the vaults, all this is most interesting and does help to demonstrate the genuine talents of these people be they psychics or 'prophetesses'. Although Apostle James might see it differently, it makes no difference where the talent originates, the function is exactly the same.

Epilogue

So many questions and so few concrete answers, but overall the consensus suggests that there is a genuine spiritual anomaly located within the walls of Rosslyn Chapel. It is regrettable that we have to use descriptive terms such as 'spiritual' that carry with them so much unnecessary baggage, but unfortunately to use more modern descriptions like 'technology' may rob what lies there of much of its importance. As we have seen, there are more people determined to deprive the building of its utterly unique status, preferring instead to include it with all the other historic, medieval buildings that dot Scotland's landscape. On one level this is acceptable, since they all make their individual contribution to the rich heritage of Scottish culture and tradition, but on another level it serves to deny and diminish the nature of this building, which, as we have seen, may be considerably more than the sum of its parts.

It has been suggested that one practical method of corroborating many of the Chapel's mysteries is to have the building professionally excavated by experienced archaeologists, something that has been attempted twice before. Unfortunately, in both cases the Rosslyn Trustees withdrew their permission for no obvious reason. When reasons were given they usually cited the Scottish rules regarding excavating graves under what is called 'Rite of Sepulchre', and permission to have this set to one side is a time consuming paper chase. The other usually quoted excuse is that digging into the sealed vaults below the Chapel flagstones might cause the building to collapse and to be fair, given medieval building practises, this assertion might well have some substance, although one might wonder that, given Sir William Sinclair's attention to detail, the foundations should be up to the standard set by the rest of the structure. Nevertheless, permission for such an in-depth excavation has ever been granted.

The use of mediums and psychics to unpick the subtle nuances shielding the secrets of the Chapel has frequently been criticised as being unscientific and preposterous, but it is my contention that they are probably the people best suited to the task, particularly if what I suspect about the designer of the Chapel is true. The old saying goes that *It takes a thief to catch a thief*, and if this is so then it takes a magician to unravel the mysteries of another magician. Make no mistake about it; the strange and wondrous talents of mediums are magical by any standards and what Sir William concealed in the fabric of his enigmatic Chapel is likewise magical. While I do not think that he actually invoked or induced the qualities present within the building, I suspect that he was well aware of the properties inherent in the location and through the design of the Chapel harnessed what was already there. As we discovered during the evaluation in October 2005, the Chapel responded to our acoustic input rather like a modern, electronic, heterodyne device, and this simply cannot be accidental.

One must ask if Rosslyn's builder did actually conceal the solution to the puzzle in the cubes decorating the ceiling of the Lady Chapel, or has this theory been grafted on like a template by a succession of seekers, all feverishly scraping away at the layers of theorising and mystery to see what lies hidden underneath? The hypothesis developed in this book relies on what I believe is depicted in the carvings decorating the faces of the cubes, viz. The Devil's Chord and what it does. What we discovered when we recreated these frequencies in the Chapel certainly indicted that something was happening, but this may be true of all medieval buildings and not just this one. We did however find a form of corroboration while the frequencies were being recreated regarding the enigmatic northeast corner and what is reputedly there; again this may have been subjective, although, if so, it was a shared, and repeatable, experience. Then of course there is the enigma of the red light. What to make of that? Does this mean that we need two sources to operate the key to revealing the secret? Always the answers remain just out of reach and with each passing year the Trustees seem ever more determined not to allow what they (perhaps rightly) consider to be off-the-wall experiments trying to unearth the secret.

This of course leaves the issue of the doorways, or, if you prefer, the vortices; are they (A) dangerous and accessible and (B) do they conceal something? The short answer to these questions is no, in retrospect they are not dangerous, nor are they easily accessible, at least not to ordinary members of the public, and even if the correct frequencies were used it is likely that it would require the talents of, once again, a fully committed and very talented medium to finally turn the key, even although it was already securely inserted in the lock. We are once again confronted with the utterly singular abilities of a class of psychically gifted people, for even among mediums it appears that, as with all skills, there are those who are more gifted and able than their colleagues. The information we received in relation to the project has been mixed; mostly positive and in one instance rather sinister, but in the main it has been encouraging. The answer to, *do they conceal something*?, is yes, they do and the likelihood is that they conceal knowledge or gnosis.

We are, however, still left with the question *if there is there a secret in Rosslyn Chapel is it what has been revealed here*? The answer to this is a definite yes on all counts. There is a secret and it is non-physical, in fact there may be more than one, but thankfully it is also the case that the answers are there too and they form part of the design and myriad carvings that are present in abundance throughout the building. Yes, there are physical attributes too; the most obvious are the knights of Rosslyn who are claimed to lie beneath the Chapel encased in their battle armour, but although these are not secrets in any real sense, they do add to the sheer gravitas of the place. There is also the possibility of the existence of an elaborate cavern system connecting a number of ancient buildings in the area. However, all the mediums concluded that what is concealed in the Chapel itself is knowledge; but it is the nature of the knowledge that presents the problem.

While there may indeed be a hidden casket containing some artefact to assist in opening the door there may be still other ways to activate it. It is my considered opinion that what we discovered relating to the sonic properties inherent in the building, and the anomaly in the northeast corner of the Lady Chapel, are major finds. Yes, there is a 'doorway' of sorts here and yes it can be opened. Equally amazing is the concept that through deliberate design the Chapel is one, vast, latent 'psychic generator' existing on the cusp of another reality, but my instincts are that that it will never be exploited to the detriment of the public, mainly because we do not fully understand the nature of this enigma. The mediums told us that Sir William was fully aware of what he was doing when he built it and as we have seen, he did it to both further man's quest for the divine and, by guile, show the Catholic Church that it was not as omnipotent or omniscient as it thought.

However, as long as human beings are fascinated by enigmas and mysteries there will always be seekers determined to unlock the puzzles that still surround us. Perhaps the best device we have available to us for unpicking the individual, and in some cases inescapably interlinked, strands of these riddles is the infinitely subtlety of the human organism. Only the incredible electrochemical processes that comprise the brain can ever hope to link with the ephemeral, unseen but totally ubiquitous world of spirituality and magic that is part and parcel of the nature of reality. Make no mistake about it, this account is of a work very much in progress and whatever else this sacred building may be, as was said at the very beginning of this book, truly, it still is *a puzzle wrapped in a mystery inside an enigma.*

References and suggested further reading:

- *The Hiram Key* (ISBN: 9780552980593) by Robert Lomas and Christopher Knight, pub Century
- *The Stone Puzzle of Rosslyn Chapel* (ISBN: 9781931882088) by Filip Coppens, pub. 2002 by Frontier Publishing
- *The Discovery of The Grail* by Andrew Sinclair pub 1999 by Arrow books
- *Rosslyn*, by Andrew Sinclair, (ISBN: 9781841585185). pub by Birlinn
- *Rosslyn*, Guardian of the secrets of the Holy Grail, (ISBN- 10: 0007332076) by Tim Wallace-Murphy and Marilyn Hopkins, pub 1999 by Element Books
- *The Holy Blood and The Holy Grail*, (ISBN: 9780099503095) by Baigent, Leigh and Lincoln, pub Arrow Books
- *The Spear of Destiny*, (ISBN-10: 0877285470) by Trevor Ravenscroft, pub 1990 by Sphere Books
- *In the Name of the Gods* (ISBN- 10: 0953993000) by David Elkington, pub, Green Man Press

Internet References

- https://en.wikipedia.org/?title=Crucifixion
- www.jewishencyclopedia.com/articles/4782-crucifixion -
- https://en.wikipedia.org/wiki/Rosslyn_Chapel
- www.scotland.org/features/rosslyn-and-the-Grail-myths
- www.sacred-destinations.com/scotland/rosslyn-Chapel
- www.britishheritage.com/scotlands-mysterious-rosslyn-Chapel/
- www.bibliotecapleyades.net/merovingians/rosslyn_Chapel01.htm
- www.slate.com/articles/life/the_rosslyn.../the_rosslyn_code
- www.rosslynChapel.org.uk/history.php
- www.crystalinks.com/rosslynchapel.html
- www.bbc.co.uk/religion/religions/.../places/rosslynchapel_1.sht
- www.youtube.com/watch?v=jqHXWXB7sKA
- www.rosslyntemplars.org.uk/index.php/rosslyn-Chapel/Grail-quest/
- www.mysteriousbritain.co.uk/.../rosslyn-Chapel-roslin-castle.ht…
- www.mythomorph.com/wp/rosslyn-Chapels-darkest-secret/ -

- www.templeofmysteries.com/rosslyn-Chapel/
- www.mythomorph.com/.../the-rosslyn-motet-rosslyn-Chapels-music-...
- www.rosslyntemplars.org.uk/index.php/rosslyn-Chapel/Grail-quest/ -
- www.geni.com/projects/The-Spear-of-Destiny/14909
- www.christianpost.com› Home› entertainment
- www.bl.uk/onlinegallery/features/mythical/Grail.html -
- www.urbandictionary.com/define.php?term=Holy+Grail –
- www.sauniere-society.org/about_us.html
- www.greyfalcon.us/Grail.htm
- www.renneslechateau.nl/2012/02/03/otto-rahn/
- https://en.wikipedia.org/wiki/Otto_Rahn
- www.secretscotland.org.uk/index.php/Secrets/SkelmorlieU-Boat
- https://www.nexusmagazine.com/.../the-mystery-of-u-33-hitler-s-secret- envo...
- archive.archaeology.org/0603/abstracts/nazis.html
- https://en.wikipedia.org/wiki/Ahnenerbe
- thirdreichocculthistory.blogspot.com/.../die-deutsche-ahnenerbe.
- supernatural.wikia.com/wiki/Grigori
- https://en.wikipedia.org/wiki/Grigory
- www.paranormality.com/grigori.shtml
- www.forensic-architecture.org›HomeLexicon Entries
- https://en.wikipedia.org/wiki/Stone_Tape
- jphaunts.com/index.php/the-stone-tape-theory

THE WORLD'S WEIRDEST PUBLISHING COMPANY

HOW TO START A PUBLISHING EMPIRE

Unlike most mainstream publishers, we have a non-commercial remit, and our mission statement claims that "we publish books because they deserve to be published, not because we think that we can make money out of them". Our motto is the Latin Tag *Pro bona causa facimus* (we do it for good reason), a slogan taken from a children's book *The Case of the Silver Egg* by the late Desmond Skirrow.

WIKIPEDIA: "The first book published was in 1988. *Take this Brother may it Serve you Well* was a guide to Beatles bootlegs by Jonathan Downes. It sold quite well, but was hampered by very poor production values, being photocopied, and held together by a plastic clip binder.

In 1988 A5 clip binders were hard to get hold of, so the publishers took A4 binders and cut them in half with a hacksaw. It now reaches surprisingly high prices second hand.

The production quality improved slightly over the years, and after 1999 all the books produced were ringbound with laminated colour covers. In 2004, however, they signed an agreement with Lightning Source, and all books are now produced perfect bound, with full colour covers."

Until 2010 all our books, the majority of which are/were on the subject of mystery animals and allied disciplines, were published by `CFZ Press`, the publishing arm of the Centre for Fortean Zoology (CFZ), and we urged our readers and followers to draw a discreet veil over the books that we published that were completely off topic to the CFZ.

However, in 2010 we decided that enough was enough and launched a second imprint, `Fortean Words` which aims to cover a wide range of non animal-related esoteric subjects. Other imprints will be launched as and when we feel like it, however the basic ethos of the company remains the same: Our job is to publish books and magazines that we feel are worth publishing, whether or not they are going to sell. Money is, after all - as my dear old Mama once told me - a rather vulgar subject, and she would be rolling in her grave if she thought that her eldest son was somehow in `trade`.

Luckily, so far our tastes have turned out not to be that rarified after all, and we have sold far more books than anyone ever thought that we would, so there is a moral in there somewhere…

Jon Downes,
Woolsery, North Devon
July 2010

CFZ PRESS

CFZ Press is our flagship imprint, featuring a wide range of intelligently written and lavishly illustrated books on cryptozoology and the quirkier aspects of Natural History.

CFZ Classics is a new venture for us. There are many seminal works that are either unavailable today, or not available with the production values which we would like to see. So, following the old adage that if you want to get something done do it yourself, this is exactly what we have done.

Desiderius Erasmus Roterodamus (b. October 18th 1466, d. July 2nd 1536) said: "When I have a little money, I buy books; and if I have any left, I buy food and clothes," and we are much the same. Only, we are in the lucky position of being able to share our books with the wider world. CFZ Classics is a conduit through which we cannot just re-issue titles which we feel still have much to offer the cryptozoological and Fortean research communities of the 21st Century, but we are adding footnotes, supplementary essays, and other material where we deem it appropriate.

http://www.cfzpublishing.co.uk/

Fortean Words is a new venture for us. The F in CFZ stands for "Fortean", after the pioneering researcher into anomalous phenomena, Charles Fort. Our Fortean Words imprint covers a whole spectrum of arcane subjects from UFOs and the paranormal to folklore and urban legends. Our authors include such Fortean luminaries as Nick Redfern, Andy Roberts, and Paul Screeton. . New authors tackling new subjects will always be encouraged, and we hope that our books will continue to be as ground-breaking and popular as ever.

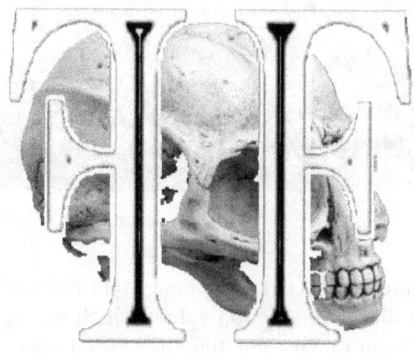

Just before Christmas 2011, we launched our third imprint, this time dedicated to - let's see if you guessed it from the title - fictional books with a Fortean or cryptozoological theme. We have published a few fictional books in the past, but now think that because of our rising reputation as publishers of quality Forteana, that a dedicated fiction imprint was the order of the day.

http://www.cfzpublishing.co.uk/